BABY BOOMER

TRIVIA

ROY ELMWOOD

About us

SPRING+STACK

Spring and Stack create modern, high-quality books designed to inspire and entertain readers of all ages. Founded by two graphic designers and artists, we bring our love of creativity and design into everything we make.

Living in the peaceful countryside of Portugal, we take inspiration from nature, adventure, and modern culture to craft books that are thoughtful, fun, and engaging. From activity books to trivia and puzzles, we aim to create something for everyone to enjoy.

springandstack.com

About the Author

Roy Elmwood is a history buff, and self-proclaimed keeper of all things nostalgic. Born in the heart of the Baby Boomer era, Roy grew up immersed in the music, movies, and cultural shifts that defined a generation. Roy can be found hiking through the countryside, perfecting his crossword skills, or sharing stories with his family and friends.

We'd Love to Hear From You!

We'd be so grateful if you could take a moment to leave a review on Amazon and let us know what you thought of this book. Your feedback helps others discover the book and keeps us inspired to create more trivia challenges!

Hey there, Boomer!

You've just been handed this book—probably as a gift from someone who thinks you remember everything from the last half-century. Spoiler alert: you won't. But that's half the fun!

This isn't just a trivia book; it's a full-blown nostalgia trip designed to test just how much of your "glory days" you've still got rattling around up there. Think you can still name the one-hit wonder behind that song you grooved to in '72? Remember which president gave us that catchphrase, or who wore the most ridiculous pants on TV? If not, don't worry—we've got plenty of reminders to jog your memory (or your frustration).

Inside, you'll find questions about the music, movies, fashion, tech, and unforgettable moments that made the 1950s through the 1990s such a wild ride. It's a little like opening a time capsule, only this one doesn't come with your high school yearbook (or that cringe-worthy mullet).

So, go ahead—flip through, quiz yourself, or challenge your friends and family. Let's see who can truly claim the title of Most Boomer of All. And don't worry, if you don't ace every question, you can just blame it on "selective memory."

Now, put on your reading glasses (don't pretend you don't need them), grab a snack, and dive in. It's time to find out... How Boomer Are You?

Good luck—and remember, no using the World Wide Web!

Contents

Okay, Boomer - Let's go!

Movie Trivia Smorgasbord: From Epics to Indies

Question 1: What 1956 film was the first epic to win an Academy Award for Best Picture?
a) *Ben–Hur*
b) *Around the World in 80 Days*
c) *Lawrence of Arabia*
d) *The Ten Commandments*

Question 2: Which indie director is known for *Pulp Fiction* and *Reservoir Dogs*?
a) Quentin Tarantino
b) Wes Anderson
c) Spike Lee
d) Sofia Coppola

Question 3: What silent film is often called the greatest movie of all time?
a) *The Birth of a Nation*
b) *City Lights*
c) *Metropolis*
d) *Citizen Kane*

Question 4: Who starred in the 1984 indie classic *Paris, Texas*?
a) Harrison Ford
b) Harry Dean Stanton
c) Robert De Niro
d) Dennis Hopper

Question 5: Which animated film was Disney's first full-length feature?
a) *Bambi*
b) *Fantasia*
c) *Snow White and the Seven Dwarfs*
d) *Pinocchio*

Question 6: What 1977 sci-fi blockbuster became one of the highest-grossing films of all time?
a) *Close Encounters of the Third Kind*
b) *Star Wars*
c) *E.T. the Extra-Terrestrial*
d) *Blade Runner*

Question 7: Which indie darling won the Palme d'Or at Cannes in 2004?
a) *Eternal Sunshine of the Spotless Mind*
b) *The Motorcycle Diaries*
c) *Fahrenheit 9/11*
d) *Lost in Translation*

Question 8: What 1994 prison drama is considered a cult classic, despite losing the Oscar for Best Picture?
a) *Forrest Gump*
b) *Pulp Fiction*
c) *The Shawshank Redemption*
d) *Schindler's List*

Answers: The correct answers are: 1. *Around the World in 80 Days* (b), 2. Quentin Tarantino (a), 3. *Citizen Kane* (d), 4. Harry Dean Stanton (b), 5. *Snow White and the Seven Dwarfs* (c), 6. *Star Wars* (b), 7. *Fahrenheit 9/11* (c), 8. *The Shawshank Redemption* (c).

Commercial Break: Memorable Ads and Jingles You Can't Forget

Question 1: Which candy's slogan was "Melts in your mouth, not in your hands"?
a) M&M's
b) Reese's
c) Skittles
d) Kit Kat

Question 2: What product used the famous jingle "Plop, plop, fizz, fizz, oh what a relief it is"?
a) Tylenol
b) Alka-Seltzer
c) Pepto-Bismol
d) Tums

Question 3: Which mascot is known for saying, "They're gr-r-reat!"?
a) Toucan Sam
b) Tony the Tiger
c) Snap, Crackle, and Pop
d) Lucky the Leprechaun

Question 4: What soda brand claimed it was "The Choice of a New Generation" in the 1980s?
a) Coca-Cola
b) Pepsi
c) Sprite
d) Dr Pepper

Question 5: The phrase "Have it your way" is associated with which fast-food chain?
a) McDonald's
b) Burger King
c) Wendy's
d) Subway

Question 6: What toy ad declared, "You can tell it's Mattel, it's swell"?
a) Barbie
b) Hot Wheels
c) Fisher-Price
d) G.I. Joe

Question 7: Which insurance company popularized the slogan "Like a good neighbor, [Company Name] is there"?
a) GEICO
b) Allstate
c) State Farm
d) Progressive

Question 8: What 1984 commercial featured the phrase "Where's the beef?"?
a) McDonald's
b) Arby's
c) Burger King
d) Wendy's

Answers: The correct answers are:
1. M&M's (a), 2. Alka-Seltzer (b), 3. Tony the Tiger (b), 4. Pepsi (b), 5. Burger King (b), 6. Barbie (a), 7. State Farm (c), 8. Wendy's (d).

Rock 'n' Roll Revolution: The Sound of the 1950s

Question 1: Who is often referred to as the "King of Rock 'n' Roll"?
a) Chuck Berry
b) Elvis Presley
c) Little Richard
d) Jerry Lee Lewis

Question 2: What Chuck Berry song became an anthem for rock music in the 1950s?
a) "Maybellene"
b) "Johnny B. Goode"
c) "Roll Over Beethoven"
d) "Sweet Little Sixteen"

Question 3: Which female rockabilly star is often called the "Queen of Rockabilly"?
a) Wanda Jackson
b) Patsy Cline
c) Brenda Lee
d) Connie Francis

Question 4: Which Buddy Holly song was famously covered by The Beatles?
a) "That'll Be the Day"
b) "Peggy Sue"
c) "Words of Love"
d) "Everyday"

Question 5: What is considered the first rock 'n' roll song to top the Billboard charts?
a) "Rock Around the Clock"
b) "Blue Suede Shoes"
c) "Heartbreak Hotel"
d) "Hound Dog"

Question 6: Which 1950s movie helped popularize rock 'n' roll with its theme song, "Rock Around the Clock"?
a) *Jailhouse Rock*
b) *The Wild One*
c) *Blackboard Jungle*
d) *Rebel Without a Cause*

Question 7: What was the nickname of Fats Domino, an influential 1950s rock 'n' roll artist?
a) "The Big Bopper"
b) "The Piano Man"
c) "The Fat Man"
d) "The King of Swing"

Question 8: What 1958 Jerry Lee Lewis song features his energetic piano playing?
a) "Breathless"
b) "Whole Lotta Shakin' Goin' On"
c) "High School Confidential"
d) "Great Balls of Fire"

Answers: The correct answers are: 1. Elvis Presley (b), 2. "Johnny B. Goode" (b), 3. Wanda Jackson (a), 4. "Words of Love" (c), 5. "Rock Around the Clock" (a), 6. *Blackboard Jungle* (c), 7. "The Fat Man" (c), 8. "Great Balls of Fire" (d).

Technological Marvels: From Automatic Transmissions to Anti-Lock Brakes

Question 1: What year saw the introduction of the automatic transmission by General Motors?
a) 1939
b) 1940
c) 1941
d) 1950

Question 2: Which car company first introduced the anti-lock braking system (ABS) for passenger vehicles?
a) Ford
b) Mercedes-Benz
c) BMW
d) Toyota

Question 3: What was the first car model to feature power steering?
a) Chrysler Imperial
b) Cadillac Eldorado
c) Packard Clipper
d) Oldsmobile Toronado

Question 4: Which automotive innovation made electric windows widely available?
a) GM's "Power-Lift"
b) Ford's "Magic Touch"
c) Chrysler's "Easy Up"
d) Honda's "Smooth Glide"

Question 5: In what decade was cruise control first introduced in vehicles?
a) 1940s
b) 1950s
c) 1960s
d) 1970s

Question 6: What was the first car with air conditioning installed as a standard feature?
a) Nash Ambassador
b) Pontiac Star Chief
c) Chevrolet Bel Air
d) Buick Roadmaster

Question 7: Which innovation, introduced in the 1980s, was crucial for hybrid vehicles?
a) Lithium-ion batteries
b) Regenerative braking
c) Direct fuel injection
d) Variable valve timing

Question 8: What technology, initially developed for race cars, became standard in high-performance vehicles in the 1990s?
a) Traction control
b) Dual-clutch transmission
c) Carbon fiber chassis
d) Turbocharging

Answers: The correct answers are: 1. 1940 (b), 2. Mercedes-Benz (b), 3. Chrysler Imperial (a), 4. GM's "Power-Lift" (a), 5. 1950s (b), 6. Nash Ambassador (a), 7. Regenerative braking (b), 8. Traction control (a).

Kennedy and Camelot: A Presidency Cut Short

Question 1: What year did John F. Kennedy win the presidency?
a) 1956
b) 1960
c) 1962
d) 1964

Question 2: Who was Kennedy's running mate in the 1960 election?
a) Hubert Humphrey
b) Lyndon B. Johnson
c) Adlai Stevenson
d) Richard Nixon

Question 3: What famous phrase did Kennedy use during his inaugural address?
a) "The only thing we have to fear is fear itself."
b) "A new frontier awaits us all."
c) "Ask not what your country can do for you, ask what you can do for your country."
d) "Let freedom ring."

Question 4: What initiative did Kennedy propose to land a man on the Moon?
a) Apollo Program
b) Mercury Program
c) Saturn Initiative
d) Lunar Leap Project

Question 5: Which Caribbean crisis during Kennedy's presidency almost led to nuclear war?
a) Cuban Missile Crisis
b) Bay of Pigs Invasion
c) Dominican Republic Crisis
d) Guantanamo Bay Conflict

Question 6: What was the name of Kennedy's domestic program aimed at progress in civil rights and space exploration?
a) The Great Society
b) The New Deal
c) The New Frontier
d) The American Dream

Question 7: Who was the alleged assassin of John F. Kennedy?
a) Lee Harvey Oswald
b) Jack Ruby
c) James Earl Ray
d) Sirhan Sirhan

Question 8: In which city was President Kennedy assassinated?
a) Houston
b) Dallas
c) Austin
d) San Antonio

Answers: The correct answers are: 1. 1960 (b), 2. Lyndon B. Johnson (b), 3. "Ask not what your country can do for you, ask what you can do for your country." (c), 4. Apollo Program (a), 5. Cuban Missile Crisis (a), 6. The New Frontier (c), 7. Lee Harvey Oswald (a), 8. Dallas (b).

The Swinging Sixties: Miniskirts, Mod Styles, and Counterculture Trends

Question 1: Who is credited with popularizing the miniskirt in the 1960s?
a) Yves Saint Laurent
b) Mary Quant
c) Coco Chanel
d) Diana Vreeland

Question 2: What iconic British model epitomized the mod style of the 1960s?
a) Twiggy
b) Jean Shrimpton
c) Veruschka
d) Penelope Tree

Question 3: What pattern was a hallmark of mod fashion?
a) Paisley
b) Polka dots
c) Chevron
d) Bold geometric prints

Question 4: Which London street became synonymous with 1960s fashion and culture?
a) Regent Street
b) Carnaby Street
c) Oxford Street
d) Abbey Road

Question 5: What group's 1967 song became an anthem for the hippie movement?
a) The Beatles – *All You Need Is Love*
b) Jefferson Airplane – *White Rabbit*
c) The Rolling Stones – *Paint It Black*
d) The Mamas & The Papas – *California Dreamin'*

Question 6: What psychedelic festival, held in 1969, defined counterculture music?
a) Monterey Pop Festival
b) Woodstock
c) Isle of Wight Festival
d) Altamont Speedway Free Festival

Question 7: Which color-block dress designed by Yves Saint Laurent became an icon of the 1960s?
a) The Modshift
b) The Mondrian Dress
c) The Twiggy Dress
d) The Pop-Art Dress

Question 8: What political protest event in 1968 became symbolic of the counterculture?
a) Paris Student Protests
b) Kent State Shootings
c) March on Washington
d) Democratic National Convention protests

Answers: The correct answers are: 1. Mary Quant (b), 2. Twiggy (a), 3. Bold geometric prints (d), 4. Carnaby Street (b), 5. The Beatles – *All You Need Is Love* (a), 6. Woodstock (b), 7. The Mondrian Dress (b), 8. Democratic National Convention protests (d).

Olympic Gold: Record-Breaking Moments from the Games

Question 1: In which year did Jesse Owens famously win four gold medals at the Olympics?
a) 1932
b) 1936
c) 1940
d) 1948

Question 2: What city hosted the first Olympics after World War II in 1948?
a) London
b) Paris
c) Helsinki
d) Berlin

Question 3: Who became the first woman to win three gold medals in track and field at a single Olympics in 1960?
a) Florence Griffith Joyner
b) Wilma Rudolph
c) Jackie Joyner-Kersee
d) Betty Cuthbert

Question 4: What swimmer won seven gold medals at the 1972 Munich Olympics?
a) Mark Spitz
b) Michael Phelps
c) Johnny Weissmuller
d) Ian Thorpe

Question 5: What was the historic achievement of Nadia Comăneci at the 1976 Montreal Olympics?
a) First gymnast to score a perfect 10
b) Youngest gold medalist in gymnastics
c) Most medals in a single Olympics
d) First female gymnast from Romania to compete

Question 6: Which country boycotted the 1980 Moscow Olympics in protest of the Soviet invasion of Afghanistan?
a) United Kingdom
b) China
c) United States
d) Canada

Question 7: What American sprinter set a world record in the 100m at the 1988 Seoul Olympics?
a) Carl Lewis
b) Ben Johnson
c) Michael Johnson
d) Florence Griffith Joyner

Question 8: In which sport did the United States perform the "Miracle on Ice" at the 1980 Winter Olympics?
a) Ice hockey
b) Figure skating
c) Curling
d) Bobsleigh

Answers: The correct answers are: 1. 1936 (b), 2. London (a), 3. Wilma Rudolph (b), 4. Mark Spitz (a), 5. First gymnast to score a perfect 10 (a), 6. United States (c), 7. Florence Griffith Joyner (d), 8. Ice hockey (a).

Walkmans and VCRs: Tech Trends of the '70s and '80s

Question 1: What company introduced the first portable cassette player, the Walkman, in 1979?
a) Sony
b) Panasonic
c) Philips
d) Toshiba

Question 2: What year was the VHS home video system introduced to the public?
a) 1973
b) 1976
c) 1979
d) 1982

Question 3: Which competitor format lost the battle to VHS in the home video market?
a) LaserDisc
b) Betamax
c) Video2000
d) CED

Question 4: What was the first commercially available movie released on VHS?
a) *The Sound of Music*
b) *Star Wars*
c) *The Godfather*
d) *Jaws*

Question 5: What feature made VCRs revolutionary for home entertainment?
a) Ability to record TV shows
b) Stereo sound
c) Compact size
d) Color compatibility

Question 6: What was the name of the first portable CD player introduced in 1984?
a) Walkman CD
b) Discman
c) Soundmaster
d) Audiophile

Question 7: Which 1980s tech trend became synonymous with aerobic workouts and fitness?
a) Walkman
b) VCR
c) Boombox
d) Cassette tape

Question 8: What company developed the compact disc (CD) in collaboration with Sony in the early 1980s?
a) Toshiba
b) RCA
c) Philips
d) Panasonic

Answers: The correct answers are: 1. Sony (a), 2. 1976 (b), 3. Betamax (b), 4. *The Sound of Music* (a), 5. Ability to record TV shows (a), 6. Discman (b), 7. Walkman (a), 8. Philips (c).

Cruising Through the Decades: The Golden Age of Ocean Liners

Question 1: What was the name of the luxury ocean liner that sank in 1912?
a) Lusitania
b) Titanic
c) Britannic
d) Queen Mary

Question 2: What year saw the maiden voyage of the RMS Queen Mary?
a) 1934
b) 1936
c) 1938
d) 1940

Question 3: Which ocean liner held the record for the fastest Atlantic crossing in the 1950s?
a) SS United States
b) RMS Queen Elizabeth
c) SS Normandie
d) MS Kungsholm

Question 4: What ocean liner became a troopship during World War II?
a) RMS Queen Elizabeth
b) SS America
c) RMS Queen Mary
d) SS Andrea Doria

Question 5: What disaster occurred in 1956 involving the SS Andrea Doria?
a) A collision with another ship
b) A fire onboard
c) An engine explosion
d) Striking an iceberg

Question 6: Which cruise line was made famous by the TV series *The Love Boat*?
a) Princess Cruises
b) Carnival Cruise Line
c) Royal Caribbean
d) Norwegian Cruise Line

Question 7: What is the term for the luxurious suites found on ocean liners?
a) Cabins
b) Berths
c) Staterooms
d) Lounges

Question 8: What modern ocean liner, launched in 2004, became one of the largest cruise ships in the world?
a) Symphony of the Seas
b) Oasis of the Seas
c) Queen Mary 2
d) Freedom of the Seas

Answers: The correct answers are: 1. Titanic (b), 2. 1936 (b), 3. SS United States (a), 4. RMS Queen Mary (c), 5. A collision with another ship (a), 6. Princess Cruises (a), 7. Staterooms (c), 8. Queen Mary 2 (c).

Poodle Skirts and Drive-Ins: Pop Culture Trends of the 1950s

Question 1: What type of skirt, often featuring appliqué designs like poodles, became a fashion icon of the 1950s?
a) Pencil skirt
b) Circle skirt
c) Poodle skirt
d) A-line skirt

Question 2: Which hairstyle was popular among teenage boys in the 1950s?
a) Crew cut
b) Pompadour
c) Beehive
d) Shag

Question 3: What snack became a favorite at drive-in movie theaters in the 1950s?
a) Popcorn
b) Hot dogs
c) Milkshakes
d) Burgers

Question 4: Which actor starred in the 1955 movie *Rebel Without a Cause*, a film that captured teenage angst?
a) Marlon Brando
b) James Dean
c) Elvis Presley
d) Rock Hudson

Question 5: What was the primary purpose of drive-in restaurants during the 1950s?
a) A convenient stop for commuters
b) A social hub for teenagers
c) A place for fine dining
d) A venue for live performances

Question 6: What dance craze of the 1950s was featured in the movie *Rock Around the Clock*?
a) The Jitterbug
b) The Twist
c) The Lindy Hop
d) The Cha-Cha

Question 7: What 1950s brand slogan declared, "Better Things for Better Living…Through Chemistry"?
a) DuPont
b) General Electric
c) Coca-Cola
d) Westinghouse

Question 8: What music genre dominated jukeboxes and defined teenage rebellion in the 1950s?
a) Swing
b) Rock 'n' Roll
c) Jazz
d) Blues

Answers: The correct answers are: 1. Poodle skirt (c), 2. Pompadour (b), 3. Popcorn (a), 4. James Dean (b), 5. A social hub for teenagers (b), 6. The Jitterbug (a), 7. DuPont (a), 8. Rock 'n' Roll (b).

Paperbacks and Pop Culture: Book Trends That Shaped the Baby Boomer Era

Question 1: Which popular paperback series, first published in the 1960s, featured the exploits of a British spy?
a) The Bourne Series
b) The James Bond Series
c) The Mission: Impossible Series
d) The Saint Series

Question 2: What genre dominated the paperback market in the 1950s and 1960s?
a) Mystery
b) Science Fiction
c) Romance
d) Western

Question 3: Which author's works, including *Slaughterhouse-Five*, became a counterculture symbol in the 1960s?
a) Ray Bradbury
b) Kurt Vonnegut
c) J.D. Salinger
d) Joseph Heller

Question 4: What company was one of the first to popularize affordable mass-market paperbacks in the U.S.?
a) Penguin Books
b) Dell Publishing
c) Bantam Books
d) Random House

Question 5: What 1970s horror novel, later made into a film, became a bestseller in paperback?
a) *The Exorcist*
b) *Carrie*
c) *The Shining*
d) *Rosemary's Baby*

Question 6: What was the name of the pocket-sized paperback guides that became popular for studying literature?
a) SparkNotes
b) Penguin Classics
c) CliffsNotes
d) Norton Guides

Question 7: Which bestselling paperback romance novelist was known for her historical epics?
a) Nora Roberts
b) Danielle Steel
c) Barbara Cartland
d) Judith McNaught

Question 8: What classic paperback was banned in several schools for its critique of conformity and authority?
a) *Fahrenheit 451*
b) *1984*
c) *Catcher in the Rye*
d) *Brave New World*

Answers: The correct answers are: 1. The James Bond Series (b), 2. Romance (c), 3. Kurt Vonnegut (b), 4. Bantam Books (c), 5. *The Exorcist* (a), 6. CliffsNotes (c), 7. Barbara Cartland (c), 8. *Catcher in the Rye* (c).

Books That Made Movies: Literary Works Adapted for the Big Screen

Question 1: What novel by Mario Puzo became a cinematic classic directed by Francis Ford Coppola?
a) *The Godfather*
b) *Goodfellas*
c) *Casino*
d) *A Bronx Tale*

Question 2: Which dystopian novel by Margaret Atwood was adapted into a film in 1990 and later a TV series?
a) *1984*
b) *The Handmaid's Tale*
c) *Brave New World*
d) *Fahrenheit 451*

Question 3: What F. Scott Fitzgerald novel was adapted into a film starring Robert Redford in 1974?
a) *The Great Gatsby*
b) *Tender Is the Night*
c) *This Side of Paradise*
d) *The Beautiful and Damned*

Question 4: Which J.K. Rowling book was the first to be adapted into a movie?
a) *Harry Potter and the Goblet of Fire*
b) *Harry Potter and the Chamber of Secrets*
c) *Harry Potter and the Sorcerer's Stone*
d) *Harry Potter and the Prisoner of Azkaban*

Question 5: What 1952 novel by Ernest Hemingway was adapted into an Academy Award-nominated film?
a) *The Old Man and the Sea*
b) *For Whom the Bell Tolls*
c) *A Farewell to Arms*
d) *To Have and Have Not*

Question 6: What movie, based on Stephen King's *The Shawshank Redemption*, became a cult classic?
a) *Stand By Me*
b) *Misery*
c) *Carrie*
d) *The Shawshank Redemption*

Question 7: What Louisa May Alcott novel has been adapted multiple times, including a 1994 film?
a) *Little Women*
b) *Good Wives*
c) *Jo's Boys*
d) *Eight Cousins*

Question 8: What Jane Austen novel was adapted into a 1995 film starring Emma Thompson?
a) *Pride and Prejudice*
b) *Sense and Sensibility*
c) *Emma*
d) *Mansfield Park*

Answers: The correct answers are: 1. *The Godfather* (a), 2. *The Handmaid's Tale* (b), 3. *The Great Gatsby* (a), 4. *Harry Potter and the Sorcerer's Stone* (c), 5. *The Old Man and the Sea* (a), 6. *The Shawshank Redemption* (d), 7. *Little Women* (a), 8. *Sense and Sensibility* (b).

Beach Getaways: From Miami to Malibu in the 1970s

Question 1: What Florida city became famous for its Art Deco architecture and beach scene in the 1970s?
a) Tampa
b) Orlando
c) Miami Beach
d) Key West

Question 2: What California beach was immortalized in the 1966 song *Good Vibrations* by The Beach Boys?
a) Venice Beach
b) Malibu Beach
c) Santa Monica Beach
d) Laguna Beach

Question 3: Which type of swimwear became a major fashion trend in the 1970s?
a) Tankini
b) Bikini
c) One-piece suit
d) Swim shorts

Question 4: What 1970s book-turned-movie depicted the carefree lives of surfers in California?
a) *Big Wednesday*
b) *The Endless Summer*
c) *Blue Crush*
d) *Point Break*

Question 5: What brand of sunglasses became iconic among beachgoers in the 1970s?
a) Ray-Ban
b) Oakley
c) Foster Grant
d) Persol

Question 6: What Hawaiian beach became a tourist hotspot in the 1970s?
a) Waikiki Beach
b) Lanikai Beach
c) Hapuna Beach
d) Makena Beach

Question 7: What water sport gained popularity on beaches worldwide in the 1970s?
a) Paddleboarding
b) Windsurfing
c) Jet skiing
d) Kayaking

Question 8: What beach town in Australia became known for its surfing culture in the 1970s?
a) Byron Bay
b) Bondi Beach
c) Gold Coast
d) Manly Beach

Answers: The correct answers are: 1. Miami Beach (c), 2. Malibu Beach (b), 3. Bikini (b), 4. *Big Wednesday* (a), 5. Ray-Ban (a), 6. Waikiki Beach (a), 7. Windsurfing (b), 8. Byron Bay (a).

Music Industry Firsts: Albums, Awards, and Iconic Moments

Question 1: What was the first album to sell over one million copies?
a) *Meet the Beatles!*
b) *Elvis Presley*
c) *The Sound of Music* soundtrack
d) *In the Wee Small Hours*

Question 2: Who won the first-ever Grammy Award for Record of the Year in 1959?
a) Frank Sinatra
b) Ella Fitzgerald
c) Perry Como
d) Domenico Modugno

Question 3: What was the first music video played on MTV in 1981?
a) "Video Killed the Radio Star" by The Buggles
b) "Thriller" by Michael Jackson
c) "Like a Virgin" by Madonna
d) "Take on Me" by A-ha

Question 4: Which artist released the first double album in rock music?
a) Bob Dylan
b) The Beatles
c) The Rolling Stones
d) Jimi Hendrix

Question 5: Who was the first woman inducted into the Rock & Roll Hall of Fame?
a) Aretha Franklin
b) Janis Joplin
c) Tina Turner
d) Stevie Nicks

Question 6: What was the first album to be released on CD?
a) *Thriller* by Michael Jackson
b) *52nd Street* by Billy Joel
c) *Dark Side of the Moon* by Pink Floyd
d) *Born to Run* by Bruce Springsteen

Question 7: What was the first rap album to win Album of the Year at the Grammys?
a) *The Miseducation of Lauryn Hill* by Lauryn Hill
b) *To Pimp a Butterfly* by Kendrick Lamar
c) *Please Hammer, Don't Hurt 'Em* by MC Hammer
d) *Speakerboxxx/The Love Below* by OutKast

Question 8: Who was the first artist to perform at the Super Bowl halftime show?
a) Michael Jackson
b) Diana Ross
c) Gloria Estefan
d) Ella Fitzgerald

Answers: The correct answers are: 1. *The Sound of Music* soundtrack (c), 2. Domenico Modugno (d), 3. "Video Killed the Radio Star" by The Buggles (a), 4. Bob Dylan (a), 5. Aretha Franklin (a), 6. *52nd Street* by Billy Joel (b), 7. *The Miseducation of Lauryn Hill* (a), 8. Gloria Estefan (c).

Civil Rights Revolution: Protests and Progress of the 1960s

Question 1: What landmark Supreme Court case ruled that racial segregation in public schools was unconstitutional?
a) Plessy v. Ferguson
b) Brown v. Board of Education
c) Roe v. Wade
d) Loving v. Virginia

Question 2: Who delivered the famous "I Have a Dream" speech during the March on Washington?
a) Malcolm X
b) Martin Luther King Jr.
c) Rosa Parks
d) John Lewis

Question 3: What 1965 legislation aimed to eliminate barriers to voting for African Americans?
a) The Civil Rights Act
b) The Voting Rights Act
c) The Fair Housing Act
d) The Freedom of Information Act

Question 4: What was the name of the 1960s student movement that supported civil rights and protested the Vietnam War?
a) SNCC
b) SDS
c) CORE
d) NAACP

Question 5: In which Southern city did Rosa Parks famously refuse to give up her bus seat in 1955?
a) Atlanta
b) Montgomery
c) Birmingham
d) Jackson

Question 6: What militant group emerged in the late 1960s as part of the Black Power movement?
a) NAACP
b) Black Panther Party
c) Urban League
d) CORE

Question 7: What university was the site of the 1962 riots over James Meredith's enrollment?
a) University of Alabama
b) University of Mississippi
c) Georgia State University
d) Howard University

Question 8: What major civil rights leader was assassinated in 1968?
a) Malcolm X
b) Martin Luther King Jr.
c) John Lewis
d) Medgar Evers

Answers: The correct answers are: 1. Brown v. Board of Education (b), 2. Martin Luther King Jr. (b), 3. The Voting Rights Act (b), 4. SDS (b), 5. Montgomery (b), 6. Black Panther Party (b), 7. University of Mississippi (b), 8. Martin Luther King Jr. (b).

Fuel Crisis and Compact Cars: Adjusting to the 1970s Energy Crunch

Question 1: What year did the OPEC oil embargo begin, leading to the energy crisis?
a) 1970
b) 1973
c) 1975
d) 1979

Question 2: What American car model was introduced as a compact alternative during the crisis?
a) Ford Pinto
b) Chevrolet Impala
c) Dodge Charger
d) Plymouth Barracuda

Question 3: Which Japanese car brand gained popularity in the U.S. due to its fuel efficiency?
a) Toyota
b) Honda
c) Nissan
d) Subaru

Question 4: What term was used to describe the U.S. economic condition of high inflation and unemployment during the 1970s?
a) Recession
b) Stagflation
c) Depression
d) Deflation

Question 5: What fuel-saving feature became standard in many cars during the crisis?
a) Cruise control
b) Overdrive transmission
c) Catalytic converter
d) Fuel injection

Question 6: Which decade saw the introduction of the Corporate Average Fuel Economy (CAFE) standards?
a) 1960s
b) 1970s
c) 1980s
d) 1990s

Question 7: What major oil-producing country stopped exports to the U.S. during the embargo?
a) Saudi Arabia
b) Iran
c) Iraq
d) Venezuela

Question 8: What was the speed limit imposed in the U.S. to conserve fuel during the crisis?
a) 50 mph
b) 55 mph
c) 60 mph
d) 65 mph

Answers: The correct answers are: 1. 1973 (b), 2. Ford Pinto (a), 3. Honda (b), 4. Stagflation (b), 5. Overdrive transmission (b), 6. 1970s (b), 7. Saudi Arabia (a), 8. 55 mph (b).

Psychedelic Sounds: Groovy Tunes of the Late 1960s

Question 1: Which band released the album *Sgt. Pepper's Lonely Hearts Club Band*, often considered a psychedelic masterpiece?
a) The Rolling Stones
b) The Beatles
c) The Doors
d) Jefferson Airplane

Question 2: What 1967 song by The Doors is a quintessential example of psychedelic rock?
a) "Light My Fire"
b) "Riders on the Storm"
c) "Hello, I Love You"
d) "Break On Through"

Question 3: What 1969 festival became the defining moment of the counterculture era?
a) Altamont
b) Woodstock
c) Monterey Pop Festival
d) Isle of Wight

Question 4: Which band's hit "White Rabbit" became an anthem of psychedelic rock?
a) Grateful Dead
b) Jefferson Airplane
c) Cream
d) Pink Floyd

Question 5: Which album by Pink Floyd is considered a cornerstone of the psychedelic genre?
a) *The Wall*
b) *The Piper at the Gates of Dawn*
c) *Dark Side of the Moon*
d) *Wish You Were Here*

Question 6: Who performed a legendary rendition of "The Star-Spangled Banner" at Woodstock?
a) Carlos Santana
b) Janis Joplin
c) Jimi Hendrix
d) Joe Cocker

Question 7: Which Grateful Dead album is famous for its long, improvisational jams?
a) *American Beauty*
b) *Workingman's Dead*
c) *Live/Dead*
d) *Aoxomoxoa*

Question 8: What song by Cream features the iconic psychedelic lyric, "In the white room with black curtains"?
a) "Sunshine of Your Love"
b) "White Room"
c) "Strange Brew"
d) "Badge"

Answers: The correct answers are: 1. The Beatles (b), 2. "Light My Fire" (a), 3. Woodstock (b), 4. Jefferson Airplane (b), 5. *The Piper at the Gates of Dawn* (b), 6. Jimi Hendrix (c), 7. *Live/Dead* (c), 8. "White Room" (b).

From the Mustang to the Camaro: Rivalries on the Road

Question 1: What year was the Ford Mustang first introduced?
a) 1962
b) 1964
c) 1966
d) 1968

Question 2: What car was Chevrolet's direct competitor to the Mustang?
a) Corvette
b) Chevelle
c) Camaro
d) Impala

Question 3: What feature of the 1969 Mustang Boss 429 made it legendary?
a) Convertible roof
b) High-performance V8 engine
c) Racing stripes
d) Dual exhausts

Question 4: What was the tagline used for the Camaro in its early advertisements?
a) "A driver's car"
b) "The Hugger"
c) "The Legend Continues"
d) "Performance Redefined"

Question 5: Which company introduced the "Pony Car" concept?
a) General Motors
b) Ford
c) Chrysler
d) AMC

Question 6: What muscle car inspired the Mustang and Camaro rivalry?
a) Dodge Charger
b) Plymouth Barracuda
c) Pontiac Firebird
d) Dodge Challenger

Question 7: What special edition of the Camaro was created for pace car duties at the Indianapolis 500?
a) RS
b) SS
c) Z/28
d) IROC-Z

Question 8: Which movie helped cement the Mustang's status as a cultural icon?
a) *Bullitt*
b) *Vanishing Point*
c) *Gone in 60 Seconds*
d) *American Graffiti*

Answers: The correct answers are: 1. 1964 (b), 2. Camaro (c), 3. High-performance V8 engine (b), 4. "The Hugger" (b), 5. Ford (b), 6. Plymouth Barracuda (b), 7. Z/28 (c), 8. *Bullitt* (a).

From Tolkien to Heinlein: Sci-Fi and Fantasy Breakthroughs

Question 1: What epic fantasy novel by J.R.R. Tolkien was first published as a trilogy in 1954?
a) *The Hobbit*
b) *The Lord of the Rings*
c) *The Silmarillion*
d) *Unfinished Tales*

Question 2: What 1961 novel by Robert A. Heinlein explored themes of free love and religion?
a) *Starship Troopers*
b) *Stranger in a Strange Land*
c) *The Moon Is a Harsh Mistress*
d) *Time Enough for Love*

Question 3: What Isaac Asimov series introduced the concept of "psychohistory"?
a) *Robot Series*
b) *Galactic Empire Series*
c) *Foundation Series*
d) *End of Eternity*

Question 4: Which Arthur C. Clarke novel was the basis for the film *2001: A Space Odyssey*?
a) *Rendezvous with Rama*
b) *Childhood's End*
c) *2001: A Space Odyssey*
d) *The Fountains of Paradise*

Question 5: What novel by Frank Herbert, published in 1965, became one of the best-selling sci-fi novels of all time?
a) *Dune*
b) *Hyperion*
c) *Neuromancer*
d) *Snow Crash*

Question 6: What term did William Gibson coin in his novel *Neuromancer* (1984)?
a) Cyberspace
b) Virtual Reality
c) Artificial Intelligence
d) Cybernetics

Question 7: What H.G. Wells novel is considered one of the first modern sci-fi works?
a) *The Time Machine*
b) *The War of the Worlds*
c) *The Invisible Man*
d) *The Island of Doctor Moreau*

Question 8: Which Ursula K. Le Guin novel introduced the world of Earthsea?
a) *The Dispossessed*
b) *The Left Hand of Darkness*
c) *A Wizard of Earthsea*
d) *Tehanu*

True Crime and Thrillers: Books That Kept Readers on the Edge of Their Seats

Question 1: What true-crime novel by Truman Capote tells the story of the Clutter family murders?
a) *Helter Skelter*
b) *In Cold Blood*
c) *The Stranger Beside Me*
d) *Mindhunter*

Question 2: What novel by Patricia Highsmith introduced the character Tom Ripley?
a) *Strangers on a Train*
b) *The Talented Mr. Ripley*
c) *Ripley Under Ground*
d) *The Boy Who Followed Ripley*

Question 3: Which Thomas Harris novel introduced the infamous Hannibal Lecter?
a) *Red Dragon*
b) *The Silence of the Lambs*
c) *Hannibal*
d) *Hannibal Rising*

Question 4: What 1974 Stephen King novel follows a telekinetic high school student?
a) *The Shining*
b) *Carrie*
c) *Firestarter*
d) *It*

Question 5: What Gillian Flynn novel became a bestseller and a hit movie in the 2010s?
a) *Sharp Objects*
b) *Dark Places*
c) *Gone Girl*
d) *The Girl on the Train*

Question 6: What legal thriller by John Grisham was his breakout bestseller?
a) *The Firm*
b) *A Time to Kill*
c) *The Client*
d) *The Pelican Brief*

Question 7: What classic thriller by Daphne du Maurier was adapted by Alfred Hitchcock in 1940?
a) *Jamaica Inn*
b) *Rebecca*
c) *My Cousin Rachel*
d) *The Birds*

Question 8: What Stieg Larsson novel begins the *Millennium Trilogy*?
a) *The Girl with the Dragon Tattoo*
b) *The Girl Who Played with Fire*
c) *The Girl Who Kicked the Hornet's Nest*
d) *The Girl in the Spider's Web*

Answers: The correct answers are: 1. *In Cold Blood* (b), 2. *The Talented Mr. Ripley* (b), 3. *Red Dragon* (a), 4. *Carrie* (b), 5. *Gone Girl* (c), 6. *The Firm* (a), 7. *Rebecca* (b), 8. *The Girl with the Dragon Tattoo* (a).

Disco Fever: Boogie Down in the 1970s

Question 1: What 1977 movie helped popularize disco music worldwide?
a) *Saturday Night Fever*
b) *Grease*
c) *Footloose*
d) *Flashdance*

Question 2: What was the name of the famous New York City nightclub associated with disco?
a) Studio 54
b) The Palladium
c) CBGB
d) The Copacabana

Question 3: Which band released the disco anthem "Stayin' Alive"?
a) ABBA
b) Bee Gees
c) Chic
d) Kool & The Gang

Question 4: What Swedish band became global superstars with hits like "Dancing Queen"?
a) Roxette
b) ABBA
c) Ace of Base
d) Europe

Question 5: Which famous disco hit starts with the lyrics, "Well, you can tell by the way I use my walk"?
a) "Le Freak"
b) "I Will Survive"
c) "Stayin' Alive"
d) "Funkytown"

Question 6: What fashion trend was closely associated with disco culture?
a) Flannel shirts
b) Bell-bottom pants
c) Leather jackets
d) Fedora hats

Question 7: What group is known for the disco classic "Le Freak"?
a) Village People
b) Chic
c) Bee Gees
d) ABBA

Question 8: What was the famous 1979 event in Chicago where disco records were destroyed?
a) Disco Inferno
b) Disco Sucks
c) Disco Demolition Night
d) End of Disco Festival

Answers: The correct answers are: 1. *Saturday Night Fever* (a), 2. Studio 54 (a), 3. Bee Gees (b), 4. ABBA (b), 5. "Stayin' Alive" (c), 6. Bell-bottom pants (b), 7. Chic (b), 8. Disco Demolition Night (c).

The Frozen Food Boom: From Fish Sticks to Pizza Rolls

Question 1: What company introduced the first commercially successful frozen dinners in the 1950s?
a) Swanson
b) Stouffer's
c) Banquet
d) Lean Cuisine

Question 2: Which frozen food item became a household staple in the 1960s?
a) Fish sticks
b) Chicken nuggets
c) Pizza rolls
d) Waffles

Question 3: What innovation in the 1970s helped expand the frozen food market?
a) Microwave ovens
b) Better packaging
c) Refrigeration trucks
d) Flash freezing

Question 4: What brand introduced pizza rolls in the 1960s?
a) Totino's
b) Red Baron
c) DiGiorno
d) Tombstone

Question 5: What frozen vegetable mix became widely popular in the 1970s?
a) Mixed greens
b) Peas and carrots
c) Stir-fry blend
d) California blend

Question 6: Which frozen dessert, introduced in the 1960s, became a nostalgic treat?
a) Ice cream sandwiches
b) Push-up pops
c) Choco Tacos
d) Frozen yogurt

Question 7: What is the name of the process that preserves food by rapidly freezing it at very low temperatures?
a) Deep freezing
b) Flash freezing
c) Quick freezing
d) Cryopreservation

Question 8: What brand slogan was "The San Francisco treat" and popularized frozen rice meals?
a) Swanson
b) Banquet
c) Rice-A-Roni
d) Lean Cuisine

Answers: The correct answers are: 1. Swanson (a), 2. Fish sticks (a), 3. Microwave ovens (a), 4. Totino's (a), 5. Peas and carrots (b), 6. Push-up pops (b), 7. Flash freezing (b), 8. Rice-A-Roni (c).

Breakfast Revolution: Cereal, Pancakes, and Toaster Treats

Question 1: What cereal was famously marketed with the slogan "Snap! Crackle! Pop!"?
a) Corn Flakes
b) Rice Krispies
c) Cheerios
d) Frosted Flakes

Question 2: Which frozen breakfast item was introduced by Kellogg's in 1964?
a) Pop-Tarts
b) Eggo waffles
c) Bagel Bites
d) Hot Pockets

Question 3: What cereal advertised itself as "Kid tested, mother approved"?
a) Life
b) Kix
c) Trix
d) Cheerios

Question 4: Which pancake syrup brand features a fictional woman in its branding?
a) Aunt Jemima
b) Mrs. Butterworth's
c) Log Cabin
d) Hungry Jack

Question 5: What iconic cereal mascot is known for saying, "They're gr-r-reat!"?
a) Tony the Tiger
b) Toucan Sam
c) Lucky the Leprechaun
d) Cap'n Crunch

Question 6: Which breakfast food was marketed as "Leggo my Eggo"?
a) Waffles
b) Pancakes
c) French toast
d) Bagels

Question 7: What cereal used the phrase "They're magically delicious" in ads?
a) Lucky Charms
b) Fruit Loops
c) Frosted Flakes
d) Cocoa Puffs

Question 8: What 1970s breakfast drink claimed to be "part of a complete breakfast"?
a) Tang
b) SunnyD
c) Ovaltine
d) Nestle Quik

Answers: The correct answers are: 1. Rice Krispies (b), 2. Pop-Tarts (a), 3. Kix (b), 4. Aunt Jemima (a), 5. Tony the Tiger (a), 6. Waffles (a), 7. Lucky Charms (a), 8. Tang (a).

DNA and Beyond: The Revolution in Biology and Medicine

Question 1: Who is credited with discovering the structure of DNA in 1953?
a) Francis Crick and James Watson
b) Rosalind Franklin and Maurice Wilkins
c) Gregor Mendel and Charles Darwin
d) Watson and Crick

Question 2: What medical breakthrough occurred in 1967 when Dr. Christiaan Barnard performed the first successful operation?
a) Open-heart surgery
b) Kidney transplant
c) Heart transplant
d) Brain surgery

Question 3: What vaccine, developed in 1955, helped eliminate polio?
a) Measles vaccine
b) Polio vaccine
c) Smallpox vaccine
d) Tetanus vaccine

Question 4: What genetic tool, introduced in 1977, allowed scientists to sequence DNA for the first time?
a) CRISPR
b) Sanger sequencing
c) Polymerase chain reaction (PCR)
d) Recombinant DNA technology

Question 5: Which virus was identified in the 1980s as the cause of AIDS?
a) HIV
b) SARS
c) H1N1
d) EBV

Question 6: What imaging technology, introduced in the 1970s, revolutionized diagnostics?
a) X-rays
b) CT scans
c) Ultrasounds
d) MRIs

Question 7: Who discovered the double-helix structure of DNA but was overlooked for the Nobel Prize?
a) James Watson
b) Rosalind Franklin
c) Maurice Wilkins
d) Linus Pauling

Question 8: What synthetic insulin, introduced in 1982, became a lifesaving treatment for diabetics?
a) Humulin
b) Novolog
c) Lantus
d) Insugen

Answers: The correct answers are: 1. Francis Crick and James Watson (a), 2. Heart transplant (c), 3. Polio vaccine (b), 4. Sanger sequencing (b), 5. HIV (a), 6. CT scans (b), 7. Rosalind Franklin (b), 8. Humulin (a).

Boxing Knockouts: The Greatest Fights and Fighters

Question 1: Who is known as "The Greatest" and won the heavyweight title three times?
a) Joe Frazier
b) Muhammad Ali
c) George Foreman
d) Mike Tyson

Question 2: What famous fight, known as "The Rumble in the Jungle," took place in 1974?
a) Ali vs. Liston
b) Ali vs. Foreman
c) Frazier vs. Foreman
d) Tyson vs. Holyfield

Question 3: Who defeated Sonny Liston in 1964 to win his first heavyweight championship?
a) Floyd Patterson
b) Joe Frazier
c) Muhammad Ali (then Cassius Clay)
d) George Foreman

Question 4: What boxer is known for the "Rope-a-Dope" strategy?
a) Joe Louis
b) Muhammad Ali
c) Sugar Ray Leonard
d) Roberto Durán

Question 5: Which fight was dubbed the "Thrilla in Manila"?
a) Ali vs. Frazier III
b) Ali vs. Foreman
c) Ali vs. Norton III
d) Frazier vs. Foreman

Question 6: Who was the first heavyweight champion to regain his title after losing it?
a) Rocky Marciano
b) Joe Louis
c) Floyd Patterson
d) Muhammad Ali

Question 7: What legendary fight ended with Mike Tyson biting his opponent's ear?
a) Tyson vs. Holyfield II
b) Tyson vs. Douglas
c) Holyfield vs. Lewis
d) Tyson vs. Ruddock

Question 8: Who is considered the best pound-for-pound boxer of all time, holding an undefeated 49-0 record?
a) Rocky Marciano
b) Floyd Mayweather
c) Sugar Ray Robinson
d) Manny Pacquiao

Answers: The correct answers are: 1. Muhammad Ali (b), 2. Ali vs. Foreman (b), 3. Muhammad Ali (then Cassius Clay) (c), 4. Muhammad Ali (b), 5. Ali vs. Frazier III (a), 6. Floyd Patterson (c), 7. Tyson vs. Holyfield II (a), 8. Sugar Ray Robinson (c).

Golden Oldies: 1960s Hits That Shaped a Generation

Question 1: What Beatles song, released in 1967, became an anthem for the counterculture?
a) "Hey Jude"
b) "Let It Be"
c) "All You Need Is Love"
d) "Lucy in the Sky with Diamonds"

Question 2: Who sang the iconic 1963 hit "Blowin' in the Wind"?
a) Bob Dylan
b) Joan Baez
c) Pete Seeger
d) Peter, Paul, and Mary

Question 3: What song by The Beach Boys epitomized the California surf culture?
a) "Surfin' Safari"
b) "Good Vibrations"
c) "California Girls"
d) "Surfin' USA"

Question 4: Which Motown group had a hit with "My Girl" in 1965?
a) The Supremes
b) The Temptations
c) Four Tops
d) The Jackson 5

Question 5: What Rolling Stones song declared, "I can't get no satisfaction"?
a) "Jumpin' Jack Flash"
b) "Paint It Black"
c) "Satisfaction"
d) "Brown Sugar"

Question 6: Who released the hit "Respect" in 1967, becoming a feminist anthem?
a) Etta James
b) Aretha Franklin
c) Diana Ross
d) Nina Simone

Question 7: What folk-rock duo released the chart-topping hit "The Sound of Silence"?
a) Simon & Garfunkel
b) Peter, Paul, and Mary
c) The Everly Brothers
d) Sonny & Cher

Question 8: What 1968 song by Marvin Gaye and Tammi Terrell became a timeless duet?
a) "You're All I Need to Get By"
b) "Ain't No Mountain High Enough"
c) "Ain't Nothing Like the Real Thing"
d) "If I Could Build My Whole World Around You"

Answers: The correct answers are: 1. "All You Need Is Love" (c), 2. Bob Dylan (a), 3. "Surfin' USA" (d), 4. The Temptations (b), 5. "Satisfaction" (c), 6. Aretha Franklin (b), 7. Simon & Garfunkel (a), 8. "Ain't No Mountain High Enough" (b).

Vietnam and the Anti-War Movement: Politics in the 1960s and 1970s

Question 1: What year did the United States officially enter the Vietnam War?
a) 1960
b) 1964
c) 1965
d) 1967

Question 2: What event in 1964 escalated U.S. involvement in Vietnam?
a) Gulf of Tonkin Incident
b) Tet Offensive
c) Fall of Saigon
d) My Lai Massacre

Question 3: What was the name of the 1968 military campaign by North Vietnam that shocked the U.S. public?
a) Rolling Thunder
b) Tet Offensive
c) Operation Linebacker
d) Ho Chi Minh Offensive

Question 4: Which famous 1969 music festival became a symbol of the anti-war movement?
a) Monterey Pop Festival
b) Isle of Wight Festival
c) Woodstock
d) Altamont Free Concert

Question 5: What 1971 document leak exposed U.S. government deception about the Vietnam War?
a) Pentagon Papers
b) Watergate Tapes
c) Gulf of Tonkin Report
d) Classified Vietnam Files

Question 6: Which Ohio university was the site of a deadly anti-war protest in 1970?
a) Kent State
b) Ohio State
c) Miami University
d) University of Cincinnati

Question 7: What was the name of the trail used by North Vietnam to transport supplies to the south?
a) Viet Cong Path
b) Ho Chi Minh Trail
c) Mekong Road
d) Hanoi Express

Question 8: What year did the Vietnam War officially end?
a) 1973
b) 1975
c) 1976
d) 1978

Answers: The correct answers are: 1. 1965 (c), 2. Gulf of Tonkin Incident (a), 3. Tet Offensive (b), 4. Woodstock (c), 5. Pentagon Papers (a), 6. Kent State (a), 7. Ho Chi Minh Trail (b), 8. 1975 (b).

Sitcom Central: Laugh-Out-Loud Hits of the 1960s

Question 1: Which 1960s sitcom featured a rural family striking it rich and moving to Beverly Hills?
a) *The Andy Griffith Show*
b) *The Beverly Hillbillies*
c) *Green Acres*
d) *Petticoat Junction*

Question 2: What 1960s sitcom followed the antics of an all-female band living in a Malibu beach house?
a) *The Monkees*
b) *The Flying Nun*
c) *The Patty Duke Show*
d) *Gidget*

Question 3: What magical phrase did Samantha use to cast spells on *Bewitched*?
a) "Abracadabra"
b) "Hocus Pocus"
c) She twitched her nose without words
d) "Presto Change-o"

Question 4: Which sitcom about an army platoon starred Phil Silvers as the scheming Sgt. Bilko?
a) *Gomer Pyle, U.S.M.C.*
b) *The Phil Silvers Show*
c) *Hogan's Heroes*
d) *MASH**

Question 5: What sitcom featured a talking horse named Mister Ed?
a) *Green Acres*
b) *Dennis the Menace*
c) *Mister Ed*
d) *The Addams Family*

Question 6: Who played the lovable Deputy Barney Fife on *The Andy Griffith Show*?
a) Don Rickles
b) Don Knotts
c) Dick Van Dyke
d) Bob Denver

Question 7: What spooky family lived at 1313 Mockingbird Lane?
a) The Addams Family
b) The Munsters
c) The Griswolds
d) The Bradys

Question 8: What sitcom followed a suburban couple trying to live a normal life despite the wife's witchcraft?
a) *I Dream of Jeannie*
b) *Bewitched*
c) *The Flying Nun*
d) *My Favorite Martian*

Answers: The correct answers are: 1. *The Beverly Hillbillies* (b), 2. *The Monkees* (a), 3. She twitched her nose without words (c), 4. *The Phil Silvers Show* (b), 5. *Mister Ed* (c), 6. Don Knotts (b), 7. The Munsters (b), 8. *Bewitched* (b).

Game Show Glory: Spin the Wheel and Test Your Knowledge

Question 1: What game show, first aired in 1956, features contestants guessing the prices of items?
a) *Let's Make a Deal*
b) *The Price Is Right*
c) *Wheel of Fortune*
d) *Jeopardy!*

Question 2: Which host is most associated with *Jeopardy!*?
a) Bob Barker
b) Pat Sajak
c) Alex Trebek
d) Regis Philbin

Question 3: What game show invites contestants to "Come on down!"?
a) *The Price Is Right*
b) *Family Feud*
c) *Press Your Luck*
d) *Deal or No Deal*

Question 4: What 1960s game show featured celebrity panelists guessing a contestant's occupation?
a) *What's My Line?*
b) *To Tell the Truth*
c) *I've Got a Secret*
d) *Password*

Question 5: What show challenges contestants to solve word puzzles by spinning a large wheel?
a) *Wheel of Fortune*
b) *Lingo*
c) *Concentration*
d) *Scrabble*

Question 6: Which long-running game show involved guessing survey responses?
a) *Family Feud*
b) *Match Game*
c) *Who Wants to Be a Millionaire?*
d) *Press Your Luck*

Question 7: Which game show featured a Whammy that would take away all your winnings?
a) *Press Your Luck*
b) *Deal or No Deal*
c) *The Gong Show*
d) *Concentration*

Question 8: What 1970s show gave contestants the chance to "trade up" for better prizes?
a) *Let's Make a Deal*
b) *The Price Is Right*
c) *Wheel of Fortune*
d) *Press Your Luck*

Breaking Barriers: Women and Minorities in Science and Tech

Question 1: Who was the first woman to win a Nobel Prize in 1903?
a) Jane Goodall
b) Marie Curie
c) Rosalind Franklin
d) Barbara McClintock

Question 2: What African American woman helped develop computer programming during her time at NASA?
a) Mae Jemison
b) Katherine Johnson
c) Dorothy Vaughan
d) Mary Jackson

Question 3: Who was the first woman to travel to space?
a) Valentina Tereshkova
b) Sally Ride
c) Mae Jemison
d) Eileen Collins

Question 4: What scientist's work on X-ray diffraction was critical to understanding DNA's double-helix structure?
a) Rosalind Franklin
b) James Watson
c) Barbara McClintock
d) Linus Pauling

Question 5: What minority scientist won the 1956 Nobel Prize for developing the transistor?
a) Ernest Everett Just
b) William Shockley
c) John Bardeen
d) Walter Brattain

Question 6: Who was the first African American woman to receive a medical degree in the U.S.?
a) Rebecca Lee Crumpler
b) Dorothy Lavinia Brown
c) Elizabeth Blackwell
d) Jane Wright

Question 7: What pioneering tech executive became the CEO of Xerox in 2009?
a) Ginni Rometty
b) Ursula Burns
c) Indra Nooyi
d) Sheryl Sandberg

Question 8: Who invented the first home security system, becoming one of the first African American female inventors to receive a patent?
a) Marie Van Brittan Brown
b) Katherine Johnson
c) Dorothy Vaughan
d) Gladys West

Answers: The correct answers are: 1. Marie Curie (b), 2. Katherine Johnson (b), 3. Valentina Tereshkova (a), 4. Rosalind Franklin (a), 5. Walter Brattain (d), 6. Rebecca Lee Crumpler (a), 7. Ursula Burns (b), 8. Marie Van Brittan Brown (a).

Who Shot JFK? The Assassination That Changed America

Question 1: What year was President John F. Kennedy assassinated?
a) 1961
b) 1963
c) 1965
d) 1968

Question 2: In which city was Kennedy assassinated?
a) Dallas
b) Houston
c) Austin
d) San Antonio

Question 3: What building was the sniper located in during the assassination?
a) Dallas Trade Mart
b) Texas School Book Depository
c) Dealey Plaza Hotel
d) JFK Memorial Tower

Question 4: Who was charged as Kennedy's assassin?
a) Lee Harvey Oswald
b) Jack Ruby
c) James Earl Ray
d) Sirhan Sirhan

Question 5: Who shot Lee Harvey Oswald on live television two days after the assassination?
a) Jack Ruby
b) Earl Warren
c) James Earl Ray
d) J. Edgar Hoover

Question 6: What was the name of the commission that investigated Kennedy's assassination?
a) Warren Commission
b) Kennedy Inquiry
c) Presidential Investigation Committee
d) Zapruder Commission

Question 7: What controversial film provided the most famous footage of Kennedy's assassination?
a) *The Kennedy Tapes*
b) *The Dealey Plaza Chronicles*
c) *The Zapruder Film*
d) *The Oswald Connection*

Question 8: What location was Kennedy's motorcade heading to when he was assassinated?
a) Love Field
b) Dallas Trade Mart
c) Texas State Capitol
d) Fair Park

Answers: The correct answers are: 1. 1963 (b), 2. Dallas (a), 3. Texas School Book Depository (b), 4. Lee Harvey Oswald (a), 5. Jack Ruby (a), 6. Warren Commission (a), 7. *The Zapruder Film* (c), 8. Dallas Trade Mart (b).

Hollywood's Golden Age: Iconic Stars of the 1950s

Question 1: Who starred as Scarlett O'Hara in *Gone with the Wind*, a defining film of the era?
a) Bette Davis
b) Vivien Leigh
c) Joan Crawford
d) Elizabeth Taylor

Question 2: What actor played the lead role in *Rebel Without a Cause*?
a) Marlon Brando
b) James Dean
c) Montgomery Clift
d) Rock Hudson

Question 3: What legendary actress sang "Diamonds Are a Girl's Best Friend" in *Gentlemen Prefer Blondes*?
a) Marilyn Monroe
b) Audrey Hepburn
c) Grace Kelly
d) Ava Gardner

Question 4: Which actor starred in *On the Waterfront* and *A Streetcar Named Desire*?
a) Paul Newman
b) Clark Gable
c) Marlon Brando
d) Humphrey Bogart

Question 5: Who became known as the "Queen of Technicolor" for her vibrant on-screen appearances?
a) Maureen O'Hara
b) Jane Russell
c) Rita Hayworth
d) Deborah Kerr

Question 6: What Hitchcock thriller from the 1950s starred James Stewart and Kim Novak?
a) *Psycho*
b) *Vertigo*
c) *Rear Window*
d) *North by Northwest*

Question 7: What movie featured Audrey Hepburn as a princess exploring Rome?
a) *Breakfast at Tiffany's*
b) *Sabrina*
c) *Roman Holiday*
d) *Funny Face*

Question 8: Who starred in *The Ten Commandments* as Moses?
a) Charlton Heston
b) Gregory Peck
c) Yul Brynner
d) Kirk Douglas

Answers: The correct answers are: 1. Vivien Leigh (b), 2. James Dean (b), 3. Marilyn Monroe (a), 4. Marlon Brando (c), 5. Maureen O'Hara (a), 6. *Vertigo* (b), 7. *Roman Holiday* (c), 8. Charlton Heston (a).

Watergate: The Scandal That Brought Down a President

Question 1: What year did the Watergate break-in occur?
a) 1970
b) 1972
c) 1974
d) 1976

Question 2: Which president was implicated in the Watergate scandal?
a) Lyndon B. Johnson
b) Richard Nixon
c) Gerald Ford
d) Jimmy Carter

Question 3: What was the name of the hotel and office complex where the break-in occurred?
a) Hilton Hotel
b) Watergate Complex
c) Waldorf Astoria
d) Jefferson Towers

Question 4: Who were the Washington Post journalists that investigated the Watergate scandal?
a) Bob Woodward and Carl Bernstein
b) Dan Rather and Tom Brokaw
c) Walter Cronkite and Edward R. Murrow
d) John Chancellor and Harry Reasoner

Question 5: What committee was being spied on during the Watergate break-in?
a) Democratic National Committee
b) Republican National Committee
c) Congressional Budget Office
d) Presidential Election Committee

Question 6: What phrase did Nixon famously say, denying involvement in the scandal?
a) "I am not a crook."
b) "I will not resign."
c) "This is a witch hunt."
d) "Fake news."

Question 7: What tapes revealed Nixon's involvement in the cover-up?
a) White House Tapes
b) Oval Office Recordings
c) Watergate Tapes
d) Executive Office Recordings

Question 8: Who became president after Nixon resigned?
a) Gerald Ford
b) Jimmy Carter
c) Spiro Agnew
d) Ronald Reagan

Answers: The correct answers are:
1. 1972 (b), 2. Richard Nixon (b), 3. Watergate Complex (b), 4. Bob Woodward and Carl Bernstein (a), 5. Democratic National Committee (a), 6. "I am not a crook." (a), 7. Watergate Tapes (c), 8. Gerald Ford (a).

Denim Through the Decades: From Blue Jeans to Acid Wash

Question 1: Which brand is credited with inventing blue jeans in the late 1800s?
a) Lee
b) Wrangler
c) Levi's
d) Calvin Klein

Question 2: What decade saw the rise of bell-bottom jeans as a major fashion trend?
a) 1950s
b) 1960s
c) 1970s
d) 1980s

Question 3: What type of denim treatment became synonymous with the 1980s?
a) Acid wash
b) Raw denim
c) Stone wash
d) Distressed denim

Question 4: Who popularized the designer jeans craze of the 1980s with provocative ads?
a) Cindy Crawford
b) Brooke Shields
c) Claudia Schiffer
d) Naomi Campbell

Question 5: What subculture in the 1950s made jeans a symbol of rebellion?
a) Greasers
b) Hippies
c) Punks
d) Rockers

Question 6: Which 1990s brand became known for its oversized denim styles?
a) FUBU
b) Tommy Hilfiger
c) Guess
d) JNCO

Question 7: What was the first brand to introduce riveted pockets for durability?
a) Lee
b) Levi's
c) Wrangler
d) Diesel

Question 8: What name is given to the process of wearing down denim for a vintage look?
a) Fading
b) Whiskering
c) Distressing
d) Sandblasting

Answers: The correct answers are: 1. Levi's (c), 2. 1970s (c), 3. Acid wash (a), 4. Brooke Shields (b), 5. Greasers (a), 6. JNCO (d), 7. Levi's (b), 8. Distressing (c).

Thrills on Ice: Hockey Heroes and Stanley Cup Showdowns

Question 1: What NHL team has won the most Stanley Cups in history?
a) Detroit Red Wings
b) Montreal Canadiens
c) Toronto Maple Leafs
d) Chicago Blackhawks

Question 2: Who was the first player to score 50 goals in 50 games in the NHL?
a) Gordie Howe
b) Wayne Gretzky
c) Maurice Richard
d) Bobby Hull

Question 3: What year did the "Miracle on Ice" occur, when the U.S. defeated the Soviet Union in the Olympics?
a) 1976
b) 1980
c) 1984
d) 1988

Question 4: Who holds the record for the most career points in NHL history?
a) Gordie Howe
b) Jaromír Jágr
c) Wayne Gretzky
d) Mario Lemieux

Question 5: Which NHL goalie holds the record for the most career wins?
a) Martin Brodeur
b) Patrick Roy
c) Dominik Hašek
d) Jacques Plante

Question 6: What team won the Stanley Cup in 1994, breaking a 54-year drought?
a) New York Rangers
b) Boston Bruins
c) Vancouver Canucks
d) Calgary Flames

Question 7: Who was the first African American player in the NHL?
a) Willie O'Ree
b) Grant Fuhr
c) Jarome Iginla
d) P.K. Subban

Question 8: What trophy is awarded annually to the NHL's best player during the playoffs?
a) Conn Smythe Trophy
b) Hart Memorial Trophy
c) Norris Trophy
d) Art Ross Trophy

Answers: The correct answers are: 1. Montreal Canadiens (b), 2. Maurice Richard (c), 3. 1980 (b), 4. Wayne Gretzky (c), 5. Martin Brodeur (a), 6. New York Rangers (a), 7. Willie O'Ree (a), 8. Conn Smythe Trophy (a).

Game Changers: The Rise of Video Games in the 1980s

Question 1: What was the first home gaming console to achieve widespread success?
a) Atari 2600
b) NES
c) Sega Genesis
d) Intellivision

Question 2: What arcade game, released in 1980, became a cultural phenomenon?
a) Pac-Man
b) Space Invaders
c) Donkey Kong
d) Centipede

Question 3: What Nintendo game introduced Mario for the first time?
a) *Super Mario Bros.*
b) *Donkey Kong*
c) *Mario Kart*
d) *Mario Party*

Question 4: What game is often credited with helping to end the 1983 video game crash?
a) *The Legend of Zelda*
b) *Final Fantasy*
c) *Super Mario Bros.*
d) *Tetris*

Question 5: What iconic handheld gaming device did Nintendo release in 1989?
a) Game Boy
b) Sega Game Gear
c) Atari Lynx
d) TurboExpress

Question 6: What was the first fighting game to introduce finishing moves?
a) *Mortal Kombat*
b) *Street Fighter*
c) *Tekken*
d) *Killer Instinct*

Question 7: What was the name of Sega's mascot introduced in 1991?
a) Sonic the Hedgehog
b) Alex Kidd
c) Crash Bandicoot
d) Spyro

Question 8: What was the best-selling video game console of the 1980s?
a) NES
b) Atari 2600
c) Sega Genesis
d) Commodore 64

Answers: The correct answers are: 1. Atari 2600 (a), 2. Pac-Man (a), 3. *Donkey Kong* (b), 4. *Super Mario Bros.* (c), 5. Game Boy (a), 6. *Mortal Kombat* (a), 7. Sonic the Hedgehog (a), 8. NES (a).

Post-War Ingenuity: Everyday Inventions of the 1950s

Question 1: What appliance, introduced in the 1950s, became a household staple for keeping food fresh?
a) Microwave oven
b) Refrigerator
c) Freezer
d) Dishwasher

Question 2: Which invention revolutionized television viewing in the 1950s?
a) Color TV
b) Remote control
c) Flat-screen TV
d) Cable TV

Question 3: What musical innovation, introduced in 1958, allowed music lovers to play entire albums?
a) Compact cassette
b) Vinyl LP
c) 8-track tape
d) Compact disc

Question 4: What popular toy, introduced in 1952, allowed kids to "build" faces on a plastic potato?
a) Mr. Potato Head
b) Play-Doh
c) Etch A Sketch
d) LEGO

Question 5: What frozen food innovation, introduced by Swanson in 1953, changed dinner habits?
a) TV dinners
b) Fish sticks
c) Frozen pizza
d) Waffles

Question 6: What kitchen gadget, introduced in 1954, became popular for brewing coffee?
a) Percolator
b) French press
c) Drip coffee maker
d) Espresso machine

Question 7: What automotive safety feature was patented in 1958?
a) Airbags
b) Seatbelts
c) Anti-lock brakes
d) Rearview mirrors

Question 8: Which household cleaning tool, introduced in 1956, made floor cleaning easier?
a) Vacuum cleaner
b) Mop bucket
c) Electric broom
d) Automatic dishwasher

Answers: The correct answers are: 1. Refrigerator (b), 2. Remote control (b), 3. Vinyl LP (b), 4. Mr. Potato Head (a), 5. TV dinners (a), 6. Drip coffee maker (c), 7. Seatbelts (b), 8. Vacuum cleaner (a).

Young Adult Revolution: Coming-of-Age Stories Across the Decades

Question 1: What 1951 novel by J.D. Salinger is considered a classic coming-of-age story?
a) *The Catcher in the Rye*
b) *To Kill a Mockingbird*
c) *Lord of the Flies*
d) *A Separate Peace*

Question 2: What 1980s film, starring Molly Ringwald, defined teen angst?
a) *The Breakfast Club*
b) *Sixteen Candles*
c) *Pretty in Pink*
d) *Ferris Bueller's Day Off*

Question 3: Which 1990s series by J.K. Rowling became a global phenomenon?
a) *Twilight*
b) *Percy Jackson*
c) *The Hunger Games*
d) *Harry Potter*

Question 4: What 1960s book by S.E. Hinton explored class conflict between the Greasers and the Socs?
a) *The Outsiders*
b) *That Was Then, This Is Now*
c) *Rumble Fish*
d) *Tex*

Question 5: What novel by John Green, published in 2012, became a bestselling YA romance?
a) *Looking for Alaska*
b) *Paper Towns*
c) *The Fault in Our Stars*
d) *An Abundance of Katherines*

Question 6: What Judy Blume book, published in 1970, addressed teenage struggles?
a) *Blubber*
b) *Forever…*
c) *Are You There God? It's Me, Margaret.*
d) *Tiger Eyes*

Question 7: What Suzanne Collins series about a dystopian future was first published in 2008?
a) *Divergent*
b) *The Hunger Games*
c) *The Maze Runner*
d) *The Giver*

Question 8: Which classic coming-of-age film follows four friends on a journey to find a dead body?
a) *Stand by Me*
b) *The Goonies*
c) *Dead Poets Society*
d) *E.T.*

Answers: The correct answers are: 1. *The Catcher in the Rye* (a), 2. *The Breakfast Club* (a), 3. *Harry Potter* (d), 4. *The Outsiders* (a), 5. *The Fault in Our Stars* (c), 6. *Are You There God? It's Me, Margaret.* (c), 7. *The Hunger Games* (b), 8. *Stand by Me* (a).

The Microwave Oven: The Gadget That Changed Cooking Forever

Question 1: Who accidentally invented the microwave oven while working on radar technology?
a) Percy Spencer
b) Nikola Tesla
c) Thomas Edison
d) George Eastman

Question 2: What year was the first commercial microwave oven released?
a) 1945
b) 1947
c) 1955
d) 1960

Question 3: What company manufactured the first microwave oven?
a) GE
b) Raytheon
c) Whirlpool
d) Frigidaire

Question 4: What was the name of the first microwave oven?
a) Radarange
b) MicroCook
c) HeatWave
d) ElectroChef

Question 5: How much did the first microwave oven cost?
a) $1,200
b) $500
c) $2,000
d) $5,000

Question 6: In what decade did microwave ovens become affordable for the average household?
a) 1950s
b) 1960s
c) 1970s
d) 1980s

Question 7: What material should never be placed inside a microwave?
a) Glass
b) Plastic
c) Metal
d) Ceramic

Question 8: What food item is famously associated with testing microwave functionality?
a) Popcorn
b) Pizza
c) Eggs
d) Bread

Answers: The correct answers are:
1. Percy Spencer (a), 2. 1947 (b), 3. Raytheon (b), 4. Radarange (a), 5. $5,000 (d), 6. 1970s (c), 7. Metal (c), 8. Popcorn (a).

Into the Atomic Age: Science and Innovation in the 1950s

Question 1: What 1951 project marked the first use of nuclear energy to generate electricity?
a) The Manhattan Project
b) EBR-I Reactor
c) Los Alamos Facility
d) Oak Ridge Reactor

Question 2: Which hydrogen bomb test was conducted by the U.S. in 1952?
a) Operation Crossroads
b) Operation Ivy
c) Operation Castle
d) Operation Argus

Question 3: What iconic science fiction film of the 1950s reflected fears of nuclear war?
a) *The Day the Earth Stood Still*
b) *War of the Worlds*
c) *Them!*
d) *Godzilla*

Question 4: What global health organization was founded in 1958 to eliminate smallpox?
a) World Health Organization (WHO)
b) United Nations Health Initiative
c) International Red Cross
d) Global Vaccine Alliance

Question 5: Who discovered the double-helix structure of DNA in 1953?
a) Francis Crick and James Watson
b) Maurice Wilkins and Rosalind Franklin
c) Linus Pauling and Erwin Chargaff
d) James Watson and Linus Pauling

Question 6: What scientific tool, invented in 1957, could detect radiation in the atmosphere?
a) Geiger counter
b) Cloud chamber
c) Gamma-ray spectrometer
d) Sputnik

Question 7: What treaty, signed in 1959, preserved Antarctica for peaceful purposes and scientific research?
a) Antarctic Preservation Treaty
b) Polar Accord
c) Antarctic Treaty
d) Southern Hemisphere Agreement

Question 8: Which Soviet satellite, launched in 1957, became the first human-made object to orbit Earth?
a) Sputnik 1
b) Vostok 1
c) Luna 1
d) Soyuz 1

Answers: The correct answers are: 1. EBR-I Reactor (b), 2. Operation Ivy (b), 3. *The Day the Earth Stood Still* (a), 4. World Health Organization (a), 5. Francis Crick and James Watson (a), 6. Geiger counter (a), 7. Antarctic Treaty (c), 8. Sputnik 1 (a).

Jet-Setters Unite: The Rise of Commercial Air Travel

Question 1: What airline introduced the first commercial jetliner, the De Havilland Comet, in 1952?
a) Pan Am
b) British Overseas Airways Corporation (BOAC)
c) Lufthansa
d) Air France

Question 2: Which aircraft, introduced in 1958, became known as the "Jet Age workhorse"?
a) Douglas DC-6
b) Boeing 707
c) Lockheed Constellation
d) Concorde

Question 3: What airline was the first to offer around-the-world flights?
a) Pan Am
b) TWA
c) British Airways
d) Qantas

Question 4: What 1970s aircraft revolutionized air travel with its two-deck design?
a) Concorde
b) Boeing 747
c) Airbus A300
d) Lockheed L-1011

Question 5: What term described wealthy travelers in the 1950s who could afford luxury air travel?
a) Sky Club Members
b) Jet Set
c) Air Elite
d) Golden Flyers

Question 6: What year did the Concorde supersonic passenger jet begin commercial service?
a) 1969
b) 1973
c) 1976
d) 1980

Question 7: What innovation in the 1960s made air travel more accessible to the middle class?
a) Budget airlines
b) Deregulation
c) Jet engines
d) Package vacations

Question 8: Which airline famously featured the slogan, "The World's Most Experienced Airline"?
a) Pan Am
b) Delta
c) United
d) Lufthansa

Answers: The correct answers are: 1. British Overseas Airways Corporation (BOAC) (b), 2. Boeing 707 (b), 3. Pan Am (a), 4. Boeing 747 (b), 5. Jet Set (b), 6. 1976 (c), 7. Jet engines (c), 8. Pan Am (a).

The Birth of Gaming: From Arcade Machines to Home Consoles

Question 1: What arcade game, released in 1972, is considered the first successful video game?
a) *Asteroids*
b) *Pong*
c) *Space Invaders*
d) *Pac-Man*

Question 2: What company, founded in 1972, became a pioneer of arcade gaming?
a) Nintendo
b) Atari
c) Sega
d) Coleco

Question 3: What game, released in 1980, became one of the most famous arcade games of all time?
a) *Donkey Kong*
b) *Pac-Man*
c) *Defender*
d) *Galaga*

Question 4: What was the first home video game console released in 1972?
a) Magnavox Odyssey
b) Atari 2600
c) ColecoVision
d) Intellivision

Question 5: What Nintendo game introduced the character Mario for the first time?
a) *Donkey Kong*
b) *Mario Bros.*
c) *Super Mario Bros.*
d) *Mario Kart*

Question 6: What handheld gaming device did Nintendo release in 1989?
a) Game Boy
b) Sega Game Gear
c) Atari Lynx
d) TurboExpress

Question 7: What game, first released in 1984, became synonymous with puzzle gaming?
a) *Tetris*
b) *Dr. Mario*
c) *Columns*
d) *Bejeweled*

Question 8: Which company introduced the Sega Genesis console in 1989, ushering in the 16-bit era?
a) Atari
b) Nintendo
c) Sega
d) Sony

Answers: The correct answers are: 1. *Pong* (b), 2. Atari (b), 3. *Pac-Man* (b), 4. Magnavox Odyssey (a), 5. *Donkey Kong* (a), 6. Game Boy (a), 7. *Tetris* (a), 8. Sega (c).

Post-War Classics: Literary Masterpieces of the 1950s

Question 1: What novel by J.D. Salinger, published in 1951, is a classic of American literature?
a) *The Catcher in the Rye*
b) *To Kill a Mockingbird*
c) *On the Road*
d) *The Great Gatsby*

Question 2: Which Ralph Ellison novel, published in 1952, explores race and identity in America?
a) *Native Son*
b) *Invisible Man*
c) *Their Eyes Were Watching God*
d) *Go Tell It on the Mountain*

Question 3: What dystopian novel by Ray Bradbury warns about the dangers of censorship?
a) *1984*
b) *Brave New World*
c) *Fahrenheit 451*
d) *The Handmaid's Tale*

Question 4: Which author's 1954 novel, *Lord of the Flies*, examines human nature and society?
a) George Orwell
b) William Golding
c) Aldous Huxley
d) John Steinbeck

Question 5: What Ernest Hemingway novel, published in 1952, tells the story of a fisherman's struggle?
a) *The Old Man and the Sea*
b) *For Whom the Bell Tolls*
c) *A Farewell to Arms*
d) *The Sun Also Rises*

Question 6: What Jack Kerouac novel, published in 1957, is considered a cornerstone of the Beat Generation?
a) *On the Road*
b) *The Dharma Bums*
c) *Big Sur*
d) *Desolation Angels*

Question 7: Which Tennessee Williams play, first performed in 1955, explores family dynamics in the American South?
a) *A Streetcar Named Desire*
b) *The Glass Menagerie*
c) *Cat on a Hot Tin Roof*
d) *The Night of the Iguana*

Question 8: What novel by Harper Lee, published in 1960, addresses racial injustice in the South?
a) *Beloved*
b) *To Kill a Mockingbird*
c) *Invisible Man*
d) *Go Tell It on the Mountain*

Answers: The correct answers are: 1. *The Catcher in the Rye* (a), 2. *Invisible Man* (b), 3. *Fahrenheit 451* (c), 4. *Lord of the Flies* (b), 5. *The Old Man and the Sea* (a), 6. *On the Road* (a), 7. *Cat on a Hot Tin Roof* (c), 8. *To Kill a Mockingbird* (b).

Grunge vs. Preppy: The Contrasting Styles of the 1990s

Question 1: What Seattle-based band became synonymous with the grunge movement?
a) Nirvana
b) Pearl Jam
c) Soundgarden
d) All of the above

Question 2: What iconic grunge accessory often featured plaid patterns?
a) Flannel shirts
b) Denim jackets
c) Leather boots
d) Trucker hats

Question 3: Which preppy clothing brand rose to prominence in the 1990s?
a) Ralph Lauren
b) Abercrombie & Fitch
c) Tommy Hilfiger
d) All of the above

Question 4: What TV show epitomized the preppy lifestyle of the 1990s?
a) *Friends*
b) *Saved by the Bell*
c) *Dawson's Creek*
d) *The Fresh Prince of Bel-Air*

Question 5: Which grunge band's album, *Nevermind*, became a defining moment in 1990s music?
a) Nirvana
b) Stone Temple Pilots
c) Alice in Chains
d) Foo Fighters

Question 6: What footwear brand was popular among grunge enthusiasts?
a) Doc Martens
b) Converse
c) Vans
d) Timberlands

Question 7: Which color palette best represents the preppy aesthetic of the 1990s?
a) Dark and muted
b) Neon and bright
c) Pastel and nautical
d) Earthy tones

Question 8: What grunge-inspired movie, starring Winona Ryder, became a cult classic?
a) *Clueless*
b) *Reality Bites*
c) *Singles*
d) *Heathers*

Answers: The correct answers are: 1. All of the above (d), 2. Flannel shirts (a), 3. All of the above (d), 4. *Saved by the Bell* (b), 5. Nirvana (a), 6. Doc Martens (a), 7. Pastel and nautical (c), 8. *Reality Bites* (b).

Trailblazing Women: First Female Achievements Across the Decades

Question 1: Who was the first woman to fly solo across the Atlantic Ocean in 1932?
a) Amelia Earhart
b) Bessie Coleman
c) Jacqueline Cochran
d) Harriet Quimby

Question 2: Who became the first female Prime Minister of the United Kingdom in 1979?
a) Margaret Thatcher
b) Indira Gandhi
c) Golda Meir
d) Angela Merkel

Question 3: Who was the first African American woman to win an Academy Award for Best Actress?
a) Dorothy Dandridge
b) Halle Berry
c) Whoopi Goldberg
d) Hattie McDaniel

Question 4: What American tennis player became the first woman to earn $100,000 in prize money in a single year?
a) Billie Jean King
b) Chris Evert
c) Martina Navratilova
d) Serena Williams

Question 5: Who was the first woman to serve on the U.S. Supreme Court?
a) Ruth Bader Ginsburg
b) Sandra Day O'Connor
c) Sonia Sotomayor
d) Elena Kagan

Question 6: Who was the first female astronaut to travel to space in 1963?
a) Valentina Tereshkova
b) Sally Ride
c) Peggy Whitson
d) Mae Jemison

Question 7: What author was the first woman to win the Pulitzer Prize for Fiction in 1921?
a) Edith Wharton
b) Willa Cather
c) Pearl S. Buck
d) Louisa May Alcott

Question 8: Who became the first female Vice President of the United States in 2021?
a) Hillary Clinton
b) Nancy Pelosi
c) Kamala Harris
d) Geraldine Ferraro

Answers: The correct answers are: 1. Amelia Earhart (a), 2. Margaret Thatcher (a), 3. Halle Berry (b), 4. Billie Jean King (a), 5. Sandra Day O'Connor (b), 6. Valentina Tereshkova (a), 7. Edith Wharton (a), 8. Kamala Harris (c).

Post-War Glamour: The Iconic Styles of the 1950s

Question 1: What style of dress, characterized by a fitted bodice and flared skirt, was popularized in the 1950s?
a) Shift dress
b) A-line dress
c) Pencil dress
d) Peplum dress

Question 2: Which designer is credited with creating the "New Look" in 1947, influencing 1950s fashion?
a) Coco Chanel
b) Christian Dior
c) Hubert de Givenchy
d) Yves Saint Laurent

Question 3: What type of shoes, featuring a narrow heel, became a staple of 1950s fashion?
a) Mary Janes
b) Kitten heels
c) Stilettos
d) Loafers

Question 4: What hairstyle, characterized by short curls, was popular among women in the 1950s?
a) Victory rolls
b) Bouffant
c) Pixie cut
d) Poodle cut

Question 5: What casual style for men, popularized by James Dean, included jeans and a leather jacket?
a) Preppy
b) Beatnik
c) Rebel look
d) Ivy League

Question 6: What makeup trend, featuring bold lips, dominated 1950s beauty standards?
a) Red lipstick
b) Nude lipstick
c) Smokey eyes
d) Blush-heavy cheeks

Question 7: What accessory, often adorned with pearls or rhinestones, completed the 1950s feminine look?
a) Neck scarf
b) Brooch
c) Clutch bag
d) Gloves

Question 8: What type of swimwear, featuring high waists and halter tops, was popular in the 1950s?
a) Bikini
b) Tankini
c) One-piece suit
d) Pin-up swimsuit

Answers: The correct answers are: 1. A-line dress (b), 2. Christian Dior (b), 3. Stilettos (c), 4. Poodle cut (d), 5. Rebel look (c), 6. Red lipstick (a), 7. Gloves (d), 8. Pin-up swimsuit (d).

Detroit's Finest: The Rise of the Big Three Automakers

Question 1: Which company is considered the oldest member of the "Big Three" automakers?
a) Chrysler
b) General Motors
c) Ford
d) Studebaker

Question 2: What innovative production method, introduced by Henry Ford, revolutionized automobile manufacturing?
a) Assembly line
b) Robotics
c) Lean manufacturing
d) Automation

Question 3: Which car model, introduced in 1927, was one of Ford's most successful vehicles?
a) Model T
b) Model A
c) Ford Thunderbird
d) Ford Fairlane

Question 4: General Motors introduced which luxury car brand in 1908?
a) Cadillac
b) Lincoln
c) Buick
d) Oldsmobile

Question 5: What Chrysler car, released in the 1950s, was one of the first vehicles to feature tailfins?
a) Chrysler 300
b) Dodge Coronet
c) Plymouth Fury
d) Imperial

Question 6: In what year did Ford release the iconic Mustang, marking the birth of the pony car?
a) 1962
b) 1964
c) 1966
d) 1968

Question 7: Which Big Three automaker launched the Chevrolet Corvette, America's first mass-produced sports car?
a) Chrysler
b) Ford
c) General Motors
d) Dodge

Question 8: What crisis in the 1970s caused the Big Three to focus on producing smaller, fuel-efficient cars?
a) The Energy Crisis
b) The Stock Market Crash
c) The Oil Embargo
d) The Steel Shortage

Answers: The correct answers are: 1. Ford (c), 2. Assembly line (a), 3. Model A (b), 4. Cadillac (a), 5. Imperial (d), 6. 1964 (b), 7. General Motors (c), 8. The Oil Embargo (c).

The Space Race: From Sputnik to the Moon Landing

Question 1: What was the name of the first artificial satellite launched into space in 1957?
a) Explorer 1
b) Vostok 1
c) Sputnik 1
d) Luna 2

Question 2: What U.S. organization was founded in 1958 to lead space exploration?
a) NOAA
b) NASA
c) DARPA
d) NACA

Question 3: Who became the first human to orbit Earth in 1961?
a) Yuri Gagarin
b) Alan Shepard
c) John Glenn
d) Valentina Tereshkova

Question 4: What U.S. program focused on sending humans to the Moon?
a) Mercury
b) Gemini
c) Apollo
d) Skylab

Question 5: In what year did the Apollo 11 mission land the first humans on the Moon?
a) 1967
b) 1968
c) 1969
d) 1970

Question 6: Who was the first person to walk on the Moon?
a) Buzz Aldrin
b) Neil Armstrong
c) Michael Collins
d) Jim Lovell

Question 7: What phrase did Neil Armstrong say as he stepped onto the Moon?
a) "One small step for man, one giant leap for mankind."
b) "To infinity and beyond."
c) "We came in peace for all mankind."
d) "The Eagle has landed."

Question 8: What was the name of the Soviet lunar program that attempted to rival the U.S. Moon landing?
a) Vostok
b) Luna
c) Soyuz
d) Mir

Answers: The correct answers are: 1. Sputnik 1 (c), 2. NASA (b), 3. Yuri Gagarin (a), 4. Apollo (c), 5. 1969 (c), 6. Neil Armstrong (b), 7. "One small step for man, one giant leap for mankind." (a), 8. Luna (b).

Luxury and Innovation: Cadillacs, Lincolns, and the High-End Revolution

Question 1: What Cadillac feature, introduced in 1912, made starting cars easier?
a) Electric starter
b) Automatic transmission
c) Power steering
d) Air conditioning

Question 2: Which Lincoln car, introduced in the 1930s, became a symbol of presidential luxury?
a) Lincoln Continental
b) Lincoln Zephyr
c) Lincoln Mark Series
d) Lincoln Capri

Question 3: What Cadillac innovation in 1948 introduced the iconic tailfin design?
a) Fleetwood
b) Series 62
c) Eldorado
d) Coupe de Ville

Question 4: Which feature, first offered by Cadillac in 1957, was one of the first automotive safety innovations?
a) Airbags
b) Cruise control
c) Seatbelts
d) Automatic headlight dimming

Question 5: What Lincoln model was prominently featured in President John F. Kennedy's motorcade?
a) Lincoln Continental Convertible
b) Lincoln Town Car
c) Lincoln Mark III
d) Lincoln Corsair

Question 6: What was Cadillac's first luxury SUV, introduced in 1999?
a) Escalade
b) Yukon Denali
c) Navigator
d) Aviator

Question 7: What high-end feature did Cadillacs in the 1950s introduce to enhance passenger comfort?
a) Automatic climate control
b) Heated seats
c) Reclining seats
d) Built-in entertainment system

Question 8: Which Lincoln innovation in the 1980s became a standard for high-end cars?
a) Digital dashboards
b) Keyless entry
c) Automatic parking assist
d) Adaptive cruise control

Answers: The correct answers are: 1. Electric starter (a), 2. Lincoln Continental (a), 3. Series 62 (b), 4. Automatic headlight dimming (d), 5. Lincoln Continental Convertible (a), 6. Escalade (a), 7. Automatic climate control (a), 8. Digital dashboards (a).

Post-War Prosperity: Rebuilding the World in the 1950s

Question 1: What plan provided economic aid to help rebuild Europe after World War II?
a) Marshall Plan
b) Truman Doctrine
c) NATO Agreement
d) Bretton Woods Agreement

Question 2: What U.S. act in 1944 helped millions of veterans purchase homes and attend college?
a) G.I. Bill
b) Servicemen's Relief Act
c) Veterans Education Assistance Act
d) Housing Recovery Act

Question 3: What international organization, established in 1945, aimed to promote peace and cooperation?
a) League of Nations
b) NATO
c) United Nations
d) International Monetary Fund

Question 4: Which Japanese company, rebuilt after WWII, became known for its innovative electronics?
a) Sony
b) Panasonic
c) Hitachi
d) Toshiba

Question 5: What 1950s event marked the start of suburban growth in the United States?
a) Baby Boom
b) Creation of Levittown
c) Highway Act
d) Post-War Housing Expansion

Question 6: What region in Germany became an economic powerhouse after receiving Marshall Plan funds?
a) Ruhr Valley
b) Bavarian Alps
c) Rhineland
d) Saxony

Question 7: What invention in the 1950s fueled consumer spending and economic growth?
a) Credit card
b) Television
c) Air travel
d) Microwave oven

Question 8: What Asian country experienced rapid industrial growth, earning the nickname "economic miracle"?
a) South Korea
b) Taiwan
c) Japan
d) Singapore

Answers: The correct answers are: 1. Marshall Plan (a), 2. G.I. Bill (a), 3. United Nations (c), 4. Sony (a), 5. Creation of Levittown (b), 6. Ruhr Valley (a), 7. Credit card (a), 8. Japan (c).

The Women's Liberation Movement: Politics and Progress

Question 1: What book by Betty Friedan, published in 1963, is credited with sparking the second-wave feminist movement?
a) *The Feminine Mystique*
b) *A Room of One's Own*
c) *Sister Outsider*
d) *Our Bodies, Ourselves*

Question 2: What landmark U.S. legislation, passed in 1972, prohibits gender discrimination in education?
a) Equal Rights Amendment
b) Title IX
c) Fair Pay Act
d) Voting Rights Act

Question 3: Who co-founded the National Organization for Women (NOW) in 1966?
a) Gloria Steinem
b) Betty Friedan
c) Eleanor Roosevelt
d) Angela Davis

Question 4: What 1973 Supreme Court decision guaranteed the right to an abortion?
a) Roe v. Wade
b) Griswold v. Connecticut
c) Planned Parenthood v. Casey
d) Brown v. Board of Education

Question 5: What slogan became a rallying cry for women in the 1960s and 1970s?
a) "Equal Pay for Equal Work"
b) "A Woman's Place is in the House"
c) "The Future is Female"
d) "Sisterhood is Powerful"

Question 6: What country became the first to elect a female prime minister, Sirimavo Bandaranaike, in 1960?
a) India
b) Sri Lanka
c) New Zealand
d) United Kingdom

Question 7: What act, passed in 1964, prohibits employment discrimination based on gender?
a) Equal Employment Opportunity Act
b) Civil Rights Act
c) Fair Labor Standards Act
d) Wage Equality Act

Question 8: What organization, founded in 1971, advocates for reproductive rights and healthcare access for women?
a) Planned Parenthood
b) Women's Health Network
c) National Women's Health Organization
d) Center for Reproductive Rights

Answers: The correct answers are: 1. *The Feminine Mystique* (a), 2. Title IX (b), 3. Betty Friedan (b), 4. Roe v. Wade (a), 5. "Sisterhood is Powerful" (d), 6. Sri Lanka (b), 7. Civil Rights Act (b), 8. Planned Parenthood (a).

Travel in the '90s: Budget Airlines and the Backpacking Boom

Question 1: Which budget airline, founded in 1985, revolutionized low-cost travel in the 1990s?
a) EasyJet
b) Ryanair
c) Southwest Airlines
d) Spirit Airlines

Question 2: What iconic travel guide series became essential for backpackers in the 1990s?
a) *Rick Steves' Europe*
b) *Lonely Planet*
c) *Frommer's*
d) *Rough Guides*

Question 3: Which Southeast Asian country became a popular destination for backpackers in the 1990s?
a) Thailand
b) Vietnam
c) Indonesia
d) Cambodia

Question 4: What budget airline introduced the slogan "Wanna Get Away?" in the 1990s?
a) JetBlue
b) Ryanair
c) Southwest Airlines
d) EasyJet

Question 5: What intercontinental transportation system was preferred by budget travelers in Europe?
a) Eurail
b) Megabus
c) Greyhound
d) FlixBus

Question 6: Which country saw a surge in budget tourism after the fall of communism?
a) Russia
b) Czech Republic
c) Poland
d) Hungary

Question 7: What popular 1990s travel trend involved staying in cheap, communal accommodations?
a) Airbnb
b) Hostels
c) Couchsurfing
d) House swaps

Question 8: What destination became a hub for electronic music lovers and backpackers in the 1990s?
a) Ibiza
b) Goa
c) Amsterdam
d) Berlin

Answers: The correct answers are: 1. Ryanair (b), 2. *Lonely Planet* (b), 3. Thailand (a), 4. Southwest Airlines (c), 5. Eurail (a), 6. Czech Republic (b), 7. Hostels (b), 8. Ibiza (a).

Board Games Bonanza: Family Fun Through the Decades

Question 1: What classic board game, introduced in 1935, became one of the most popular family games of all time?
a) *Clue*
b) *Scrabble*
c) *Monopoly*
d) *Risk*

Question 2: Which word-based board game, created in 1948, challenges players to form words on a grid?
a) *Boggle*
b) *Scattergories*
c) *Scrabble*
d) *Pictionary*

Question 3: What board game, launched in 1965, is known for its spinner and life-themed gameplay?
a) *Candy Land*
b) *The Game of Life*
c) *Trouble*
d) *Sorry!*

Question 4: Which game, introduced in the 1970s, involves world domination through strategic battles?
a) *Axis & Allies*
b) *Risk*
c) *Stratego*
d) *Diplomacy*

Question 5: What 1980s board game, based on a mystery theme, asks players to solve a murder?
a) *Clue*
b) *Mastermind*
c) *Guess Who?*
d) *Taboo*

Question 6: What colorful board game for young children was first introduced in 1949?
a) *Candy Land*
b) *Chutes and Ladders*
c) *Hi Ho! Cherry-O*
d) *Cootie*

Question 7: What trivia-based board game, released in 1981, became a cultural phenomenon?
a) *Jeopardy!*
b) *Trivial Pursuit*
c) *Scattergories*
d) *Outburst*

Question 8: Which fast-paced word-guessing game, introduced in 1985, uses a drawing pad?
a) *Taboo*
b) *Pictionary*
c) *Scattergories*
d) *Balderdash*

Answers: The correct answers are: 1. *Monopoly* (c), 2. *Scrabble* (c), 3. *The Game of Life* (b), 4. *Risk* (b), 5. *Clue* (a), 6. *Candy Land* (a), 7. *Trivial Pursuit* (b), 8. *Pictionary* (b).

Broadcast Beginnings: Firsts in Radio, TV, and News Media

Question 1: What year did the first commercial radio broadcast occur in the United States?
a) 1919
b) 1920
c) 1922
d) 1925

Question 2: Which was the first American radio station to go on air?
a) KDKA
b) WGN
c) WOR
d) NBC

Question 3: What was the first television station to air a regular schedule in 1939?
a) CBS
b) NBC
c) ABC
d) DuMont

Question 4: What 1950s news anchor was one of the most trusted figures in American broadcasting?
a) Walter Cronkite
b) Edward R. Murrow
c) Dan Rather
d) Chet Huntley

Question 5: What 1940s radio show became one of the first TV sitcoms?
a) *I Love Lucy*
b) *The Goldbergs*
c) *The Honeymooners*
d) *Leave It to Beaver*

Question 6: What was the name of the first televised presidential debate in 1960?
a) Eisenhower vs. Stevenson
b) Nixon vs. Kennedy
c) Johnson vs. Goldwater
d) Carter vs. Ford

Question 7: Which international news channel launched in 1980, providing 24-hour news coverage?
a) BBC News
b) Fox News
c) CNN
d) MSNBC

Question 8: What 1938 radio broadcast by Orson Welles caused mass panic by simulating a Martian invasion?
a) *The War of the Worlds*
b) *Mars Attacks!*
c) *The Day the Earth Stood Still*
d) *Contact*

Answers: The correct answers are: 1. 1920 (b), 2. KDKA (a), 3. NBC (b), 4. Edward R. Murrow (b), 5. *The Goldbergs* (b), 6. Nixon vs. Kennedy (b), 7. CNN (c), 8. *The War of the Worlds* (a).

Got Milk? Advertising Catchphrases That Stuck

Question 1: What brand popularized the slogan "Breakfast of Champions"?
a) Wheaties
b) Cheerios
c) Corn Flakes
d) Frosted Flakes

Question 2: Which brand is known for the slogan "Just Do It"?
a) Reebok
b) Nike
c) Adidas
d) Under Armour

Question 3: What candy used the tagline "Melts in your mouth, not in your hands"?
a) Reese's Pieces
b) Skittles
c) M&M's
d) Snickers

Question 4: Which fast-food chain famously asked, "Where's the beef?" in the 1980s?
a) McDonald's
b) Wendy's
c) Burger King
d) Arby's

Question 5: What soft drink was advertised with the phrase "It's the real thing"?
a) Pepsi
b) Coca-Cola
c) Dr Pepper
d) Sprite

Question 6: Which beer brand used the tagline "This Bud's for you"?
a) Budweiser
b) Coors Light
c) Miller Lite
d) Heineken

Question 7: What car company's slogan was "The ultimate driving machine"?
a) Mercedes-Benz
b) BMW
c) Audi
d) Lexus

Question 8: Which dairy campaign used the iconic slogan "Got Milk?"
a) Dairy Farmers of America
b) California Milk Processor Board
c) American Dairy Association
d) National Dairy Council

Answers: The correct answers are: 1. Wheaties (a), 2. Nike (b), 3. M&M's (c), 4. Wendy's (b), 5. Coca-Cola (b), 6. Budweiser (a), 7. BMW (b), 8. California Milk Processor Board (b).

Haute Couture Icons: The Designers Who Defined the Baby Boomer Era

Question 1: Which designer introduced the "New Look" in 1947, revolutionizing women's fashion in the 1950s?
a) Coco Chanel
b) Christian Dior
c) Yves Saint Laurent
d) Hubert de Givenchy

Question 2: Which iconic designer popularized the little black dress?
a) Coco Chanel
b) Elsa Schiaparelli
c) Jeanne Lanvin
d) Madeleine Vionnet

Question 3: Which designer is credited with inventing the miniskirt in the 1960s?
a) Mary Quant
b) Pierre Cardin
c) André Courrèges
d) Vivienne Westwood

Question 4: Who was the founder of the Givenchy fashion house, known for dressing Audrey Hepburn?
a) Hubert de Givenchy
b) Valentino Garavani
c) Oscar de la Renta
d) Karl Lagerfeld

Question 5: Which American designer became famous for glamorous 1950s evening wear?
a) Halston
b) Oleg Cassini
c) Charles James
d) Norman Norell

Question 6: What designer introduced futuristic and space-age fashion in the 1960s?
a) Paco Rabanne
b) Pierre Cardin
c) Emilio Pucci
d) Balenciaga

Question 7: Who was the first African American designer to gain widespread acclaim in the 1970s?
a) Stephen Burrows
b) Willi Smith
c) Ann Lowe
d) Dapper Dan

Question 8: Which Italian designer founded a luxury brand in the 1970s and became synonymous with opulence?
a) Giorgio Armani
b) Gianni Versace
c) Dolce & Gabbana
d) Salvatore Ferragamo

Answers: The correct answers are: 1. Christian Dior (b), 2. Coco Chanel (a), 3. Mary Quant (a), 4. Hubert de Givenchy (a), 5. Charles James (c), 6. Pierre Cardin (b), 7. Stephen Burrows (a), 8. Gianni Versace (b).

Comfort Food Classics: Dishes That Defined the 1950s

Question 1: What casserole, made with green beans and crispy fried onions, became a 1950s classic?
a) Tuna casserole
b) Green bean casserole
c) Mac and cheese bake
d) Potato gratin

Question 2: What gelatin dessert, often molded into elaborate shapes, was a popular party dish?
a) Jell-O salad
b) Ambrosia
c) Panna cotta
d) Fruit compote

Question 3: Which canned meat became a household staple during the 1950s?
a) Corned beef
b) Spam
c) Deviled ham
d) Vienna sausages

Question 4: What comfort food dish features creamy mashed potatoes topped with browned ground beef and vegetables?
a) Shepherd's pie
b) Pot pie
c) Meatloaf
d) Salisbury steak

Question 5: What frozen treat, served on a stick, became a hit in the 1950s?
a) Popsicles
b) Ice cream bars
c) Creamsicles
d) Klondike bars

Question 6: What breakfast dish, featuring sausage links wrapped in pancakes, gained popularity in the 1950s?
a) Pigs in a blanket
b) Corn dogs
c) Sausage rolls
d) Pancake dogs

Question 7: What type of pie, made with a chocolate filling, became a diner favorite?
a) Lemon meringue pie
b) Banana cream pie
c) Boston cream pie
d) Chocolate silk pie

Question 8: Which 1950s dish combined marshmallows, pineapple, and whipped cream?
a) Watergate salad
b) Ambrosia
c) Fluff salad
d) Waldorf salad

Answers: The correct answers are: 1. Green bean casserole (b), 2. Jell-O salad (a), 3. Spam (b), 4. Shepherd's pie (a), 5. Creamsicles (c), 6. Pigs in a blanket (a), 7. Chocolate silk pie (d), 8. Ambrosia (b).

The Beat Generation: Writers, Thinkers, and Rebels of the 1950s

Question 1: Which Jack Kerouac novel became the defining work of the Beat Generation?
a) *Big Sur*
b) *The Dharma Bums*
c) *On the Road*
d) *Desolation Angels*

Question 2: What Allen Ginsberg poem, published in 1956, became a landmark of Beat literature?
a) *Howl*
b) *Kaddish*
c) *America*
d) *Sunflower Sutra*

Question 3: Which Beat writer authored *Naked Lunch*, a controversial novel exploring addiction?
a) Jack Kerouac
b) Allen Ginsberg
c) William S. Burroughs
d) Neal Cassady

Question 4: What city was considered the birthplace of the Beat movement?
a) San Francisco
b) New York City
c) Los Angeles
d) Chicago

Question 5: Which literary figure is often referred to as the "spiritual godfather" of the Beats?
a) Henry Miller
b) Walt Whitman
c) Kenneth Rexroth
d) Ezra Pound

Question 6: What Beat Generation figure was immortalized as Dean Moriarty in *On the Road*?
a) Neal Cassady
b) Allen Ginsberg
c) William S. Burroughs
d) Gary Snyder

Question 7: What group, founded by Ginsberg and others, read poetry at San Francisco's Six Gallery in 1955?
a) The Black Mountain Poets
b) The New York School
c) The Six Gallery Poets
d) The San Francisco Renaissance

Question 8: What Buddhist themes are explored in Jack Kerouac's *The Dharma Bums*?
a) Enlightenment and nature
b) Love and rebellion
c) War and peace
d) Urban alienation

Answers: The correct answers are: 1. *On the Road* (c), 2. *Howl* (a), 3. William S. Burroughs (c), 4. San Francisco (a), 5. Kenneth Rexroth (c), 6. Neal Cassady (a), 7. The Six Gallery Poets (c), 8. Enlightenment and nature (a).

Jingles You Can't Forget: Catchy Tunes of the '60s and '70s

Question 1: What candy used the jingle "Sometimes you feel like a nut, sometimes you don't"?
a) Reese's
b) Almond Joy and Mounds
c) Milky Way
d) Snickers

Question 2: Which soda brand featured the famous "I'd Like to Buy the World a Coke" jingle?
a) Pepsi
b) Coca-Cola
c) Dr Pepper
d) RC Cola

Question 3: What 1970s toy commercial used the jingle "It's slinky, it's slinky"?
a) Etch A Sketch
b) Hula Hoop
c) Slinky
d) Mr. Potato Head

Question 4: Which fast-food chain introduced the jingle "Two all-beef patties, special sauce, lettuce, cheese…" in the 1970s?
a) Burger King
b) McDonald's
c) Wendy's
d) Arby's

Question 5: What iconic battery brand used the slogan "It keeps going and going…" in the 1970s?
a) Duracell
b) Rayovac
c) Energizer
d) Eveready

Question 6: Which brand promoted its bologna with the catchy "My bologna has a first name…" jingle?
a) Oscar Mayer
b) Hillshire Farm
c) Ball Park
d) Armour

Question 7: What 1960s cereal ad sang the tune, "They're magically delicious"?
a) Lucky Charms
b) Frosted Flakes
c) Cheerios
d) Froot Loops

Question 8: What laundry detergent used the jingle "Ring around the collar" in its commercials?
a) Tide
b) Wisk
c) Cheer
d) Gain

Answers: The correct answers are:
1. Almond Joy and Mounds (b),
2. Coca-Cola (b), 3. Slinky (c), 4.
McDonald's (b), 5. Energizer (c), 6.
Oscar Mayer (a), 7. Lucky Charms
(a), 8. Wisk (b).

Technology Takes Over: The Digital Revolution of the 1990s

Question 1: What search engine, founded in 1998, eventually became a tech giant?
a) Yahoo!
b) Google
c) Bing
d) AltaVista

Question 2: What portable music device did Sony release in the early 1990s?
a) Walkman
b) Discman
c) MP3 Player
d) iPod

Question 3: Which social media platform, launched in 1997, is considered one of the first?
a) MySpace
b) Friendster
c) SixDegrees
d) Facebook

Question 4: What operating system, introduced in 1995, changed the personal computer industry?
a) Linux
b) Windows 95
c) macOS
d) MS-DOS

Question 5: What iconic internet sound came from connecting through dial-up modems?
a) Beeping
b) Buzzing
c) Screeching
d) Clicking

Question 6: What was the name of the first widely used web browser, launched in 1993?
a) Mosaic
b) Netscape Navigator
c) Internet Explorer
d) Opera

Question 7: Which e-commerce site, founded in 1994, started as an online bookstore?
a) Amazon
b) eBay
c) Barnes & Noble
d) Overstock

Question 8: What online messaging service, popular in the 1990s, used screen names and AIM?
a) Yahoo! Messenger
b) AOL Instant Messenger
c) ICQ
d) MSN Messenger

Answers: The correct answers are: 1. Google (b), 2. Discman (b), 3. SixDegrees (c), 4. Windows 95 (b), 5. Screeching (c), 6. Mosaic (a), 7. Amazon (a), 8. AOL Instant Messenger (b).

Watergate and Resignation: Nixon's Scandal and Legacy

Question 1: What year did the Watergate break-in occur?
a) 1970
b) 1972
c) 1973
d) 1974

Question 2: What hotel and office complex was the site of the break-in?
a) The Pentagon
b) The Capitol
c) The Watergate Complex
d) The Jefferson Building

Question 3: Which U.S. president was implicated in the Watergate scandal?
a) Lyndon B. Johnson
b) Gerald Ford
c) Richard Nixon
d) Jimmy Carter

Question 4: What phrase did Nixon use to deny his involvement in Watergate?
a) "I am not a crook."
b) "I will not resign."
c) "This is a witch hunt."
d) "The truth will prevail."

Question 5: Who were the two Washington Post reporters that uncovered much of the Watergate story?
a) Walter Cronkite and Dan Rather
b) Bob Woodward and Carl Bernstein
c) Edward R. Murrow and Chet Huntley
d) Peter Jennings and Tom Brokaw

Question 6: What tapes revealed Nixon's involvement in the Watergate cover-up?
a) Oval Office Tapes
b) Watergate Tapes
c) White House Recordings
d) Executive Conversations

Question 7: What year did Nixon resign from the presidency?
a) 1973
b) 1974
c) 1975
d) 1976

Question 8: Who became president immediately after Nixon resigned?
a) Jimmy Carter
b) Spiro Agnew
c) Gerald Ford
d) Ronald Reagan

Answers: The correct answers are: 1. 1972 (b), 2. The Watergate Complex (c), 3. Richard Nixon (c), 4. "I am not a crook." (a), 5. Bob Woodward and Carl Bernstein (b), 6. Watergate Tapes (b), 7. 1974 (b), 8. Gerald Ford (c).

Saturday Morning Favorites: Cartoons and Comic Books

Question 1: Which animated series, featuring Fred, Wilma, and Dino, was the first prime-time cartoon?
a) *The Flintstones*
b) *The Jetsons*
c) *Scooby-Doo, Where Are You!*
d) *Yogi Bear*

Question 2: What superhero team made their comic book debut in *The Brave and the Bold #28* in 1960?
a) The Avengers
b) The X-Men
c) Justice League of America
d) The Fantastic Four

Question 3: What cartoon dog and his gang of mystery-solving friends first aired in 1969?
a) Huckleberry Hound
b) Scooby-Doo
c) Muttley
d) Droopy

Question 4: What 1950s comic strip featured the characters Charlie Brown, Snoopy, and Linus?
a) *Peanuts*
b) *Garfield*
c) *Calvin and Hobbes*
d) *Blondie*

Question 5: Which superhero received his first animated TV series in 1966?
a) Superman
b) Spider-Man
c) Batman
d) The Hulk

Question 6: What Hanna-Barbera cartoon featured a prehistoric family living in Bedrock?
a) *The Jetsons*
b) *The Flintstones*
c) *Jonny Quest*
d) *Top Cat*

Question 7: Which iconic Saturday morning cartoon featured the tagline "More than meets the eye"?
a) *Transformers*
b) *G.I. Joe*
c) *He-Man and the Masters of the Universe*
d) *Thundercats*

Question 8: What DC Comics superhero was famously portrayed by Lynda Carter in the 1970s TV series?
a) Wonder Woman
b) Supergirl
c) Batgirl
d) Zatanna

Answers: The correct answers are: 1. *The Flintstones* (a), 2. Justice League of America (c), 3. Scooby-Doo (b), 4. *Peanuts* (a), 5. Spider-Man (b), 6. *The Flintstones* (b), 7. *Transformers* (a), 8. Wonder Woman (a).

The Pulitzer Winners: Prize-Winning Literature from the 1950s to the 1990s

Question 1: What novel by Harper Lee won the Pulitzer Prize for Fiction in 1961?
a) *To Kill a Mockingbird*
b) *The Catcher in the Rye*
c) *Invisible Man*
d) *A Separate Peace*

Question 2: Which Toni Morrison novel, exploring the legacy of slavery, won the Pulitzer in 1988?
a) *Beloved*
b) *Song of Solomon*
c) *The Bluest Eye*
d) *Jazz*

Question 3: What novel by John Steinbeck, published in 1952, won a Pulitzer Prize for its portrayal of migrant workers?
a) *Of Mice and Men*
b) *The Grapes of Wrath*
c) *East of Eden*
d) *Travels with Charley*

Question 4: What Alice Walker novel, depicting the struggles of African American women, won the Pulitzer in 1983?
a) *Meridian*
b) *The Color Purple*
c) *In Search of Our Mothers' Gardens*
d) *By the Light of My Father's Smile*

Question 5: Which Michael Shaara book about the Battle of Gettysburg won the Pulitzer in 1975?
a) *The Killer Angels*
b) *Gone for Soldiers*
c) *Gods and Generals*
d) *The Last Full Measure*

Question 6: Which Anne Tyler novel, about an unassuming man's life, won the Pulitzer in 1989?
a) *Dinner at the Homesick Restaurant*
b) *The Accidental Tourist*
c) *Breathing Lessons*
d) *Back When We Were Grownups*

Question 7: What Eudora Welty book, a collection of short stories, won the Pulitzer in 1973?
a) *The Optimist's Daughter*
b) *Delta Wedding*
c) *Losing Battles*
d) *The Golden Apples*

Question 8: Which William Kennedy novel, set in Albany, won the Pulitzer in 1984?
a) *Ironweed*
b) *Billy Phelan's Greatest Game*
c) *Legs*
d) *Roscoe*

Answers: The correct answers are: 1. *To Kill a Mockingbird* (a), 2. *Beloved* (a), 3. *East of Eden* (c), 4. *The Color Purple* (b), 5. *The Killer Angels* (a), 6. *Breathing Lessons* (c), 7. *The Optimist's Daughter* (a), 8. *Ironweed* (a).

Cigarettes and Soap: Controversial Ads of the Baby Boomer Era

Question 1: What cigarette brand used the slogan "Reach for a Lucky instead of a sweet"?
a) Lucky Strike
b) Marlboro
c) Camel
d) Pall Mall

Question 2: Which soap brand advertised itself as "99 and 44/100% pure"?
a) Dove
b) Ivory
c) Palmolive
d) Lifebuoy

Question 3: What cigarette brand introduced the rugged "Marlboro Man" in the 1950s?
a) Camel
b) Marlboro
c) Chesterfield
d) Parliament

Question 4: What brand used the tagline "You've come a long way, baby" to target women smokers?
a) Virginia Slims
b) Capri
c) Salem
d) Merit

Question 5: Which detergent brand claimed it could clean "ring around the collar"?
a) Tide
b) Wisk
c) Cheer
d) Oxydol

Question 6: What cigarette company claimed to be "The doctor's choice" in early advertisements?
a) Chesterfield
b) Camel
c) Pall Mall
d) Kool

Question 7: Which soap brand's ad featured a baby and emphasized its mildness for skin?
a) Ivory
b) Dove
c) Johnson's Baby Soap
d) Palmolive

Question 8: What cigarette slogan advertised "More doctors smoke [our brand]"?
a) Camel
b) Lucky Strike
c) Marlboro
d) Old Gold

Answers: The correct answers are: 1. Lucky Strike (a), 2. Ivory (b), 3. Marlboro (b), 4. Virginia Slims (a), 5. Wisk (b), 6. Camel (b), 7. Johnson's Baby Soap (c), 8. Camel (a).

The Race to Space: Milestones of the Space Age

Question 1: What was the name of the first artificial satellite launched into space in 1957?
a) Explorer 1
b) Sputnik 1
c) Vostok 1
d) Luna 2

Question 2: Who was the first human to orbit Earth in 1961?
a) Alan Shepard
b) Yuri Gagarin
c) John Glenn
d) Valentina Tereshkova

Question 3: What U.S. spacecraft carried the first American into space in 1961?
a) Freedom 7
b) Mercury-Atlas 6
c) Apollo 11
d) Gemini 3

Question 4: What year did the Apollo 11 mission land the first humans on the Moon?
a) 1967
b) 1968
c) 1969
d) 1970

Question 5: What phrase did Neil Armstrong famously say as he stepped onto the Moon?
a) "The Eagle has landed."
b) "We came in peace for all mankind."
c) "One small step for man, one giant leap for mankind."
d) "To infinity and beyond!"

Question 6: What was the first U.S. space station, launched in 1973?
a) Skylab
b) ISS
c) Mir
d) Gemini Station

Question 7: Which shuttle became the first reusable spacecraft in 1981?
a) Challenger
b) Discovery
c) Columbia
d) Atlantis

Question 8: What international space project was launched in 1998 and is still operational today?
a) Skylab
b) Hubble Space Telescope
c) International Space Station (ISS)
d) Galileo Orbiter

Answers: The correct answers are: 1. Sputnik 1 (b), 2. Yuri Gagarin (b), 3. Freedom 7 (a), 4. 1969 (c), 5. "One small step for man, one giant leap for mankind." (c), 6. Skylab (a), 7. Columbia (c), 8. International Space Station (c).

Sports Cars of the '80s and '90s: Sleek, Fast, and Furious

Question 1: What iconic Ferrari model, introduced in 1987, was one of the fastest cars of its time?
a) Ferrari 308 GTB
b) Ferrari F40
c) Ferrari Testarossa
d) Ferrari 512 BB

Question 2: What Japanese sports car, launched in the 1990s, gained fame for its performance and appearances in *The Fast and the Furious*?
a) Mazda RX-7
b) Nissan Skyline GT-R
c) Toyota Supra
d) Mitsubishi 3000GT

Question 3: What American car, introduced in 1992, featured a bold design and a V10 engine?
a) Dodge Viper
b) Chevrolet Corvette ZR-1
c) Ford Mustang SVT Cobra
d) Pontiac Firebird

Question 4: Which Porsche model, first introduced in 1984, set a new standard for luxury sports cars?
a) Porsche 911 Carrera
b) Porsche 944 Turbo
c) Porsche 928
d) Porsche Boxster

Question 5: What Italian sports car maker introduced the Diablo in 1990?
a) Lamborghini
b) Ferrari
c) Maserati
d) Pagani

Question 6: Which British car company launched the McLaren F1 in 1992, one of the fastest production cars of all time?
a) Lotus
b) Aston Martin
c) McLaren
d) Jaguar

Question 7: What lightweight Japanese roadster became a sensation in 1989?
a) Toyota MR2
b) Honda S2000
c) Mazda MX-5 Miata
d) Subaru BRZ

Question 8: What iconic Chevrolet sports car entered its fourth generation (C4) in the 1980s?
a) Chevrolet Camaro
b) Chevrolet Corvette
c) Chevrolet Impala
d) Chevrolet Malibu

Answers: The correct answers are: 1. Ferrari F40 (b), 2. Toyota Supra (c), 3. Dodge Viper (a), 4. Porsche 911 Carrera (a), 5. Lamborghini (a), 6. McLaren (c), 7. Mazda MX-5 Miata (c), 8. Chevrolet Corvette (b).

Historic Events That Shook the World: Famous Firsts in Global History

Question 1: Who was the first person to sail around the world?
a) Christopher Columbus
b) Ferdinand Magellan
c) Vasco da Gama
d) Sir Francis Drake

Question 2: What year did women in the United States gain the right to vote?
a) 1918
b) 1920
c) 1925
d) 1930

Question 3: What was the first man-made object to reach space in 1957?
a) Sputnik 1
b) Explorer 1
c) Luna 1
d) Vostok 1

Question 4: Who was the first woman to fly solo across the Atlantic Ocean?
a) Amelia Earhart
b) Bessie Coleman
c) Jacqueline Cochran
d) Valentina Tereshkova

Question 5: What was the first country to legalize same-sex marriage in 2001?
a) Canada
b) Netherlands
c) Denmark
d) Sweden

Question 6: What was the first city to host the modern Olympic Games in 1896?
a) London
b) Paris
c) Athens
d) Berlin

Question 7: What was the first animal sent into space in 1957?
a) A monkey
b) A dog named Laika
c) A mouse
d) A chimpanzee

Question 8: Who was the first African American President of the United States?
a) Barack Obama
b) Jesse Jackson
c) Colin Powell
d) Shirley Chisholm

Answers: The correct answers are: 1. Ferdinand Magellan (b), 2. 1920 (b), 3. Sputnik 1 (a), 4. Amelia Earhart (a), 5. Netherlands (b), 6. Athens (c), 7. A dog named Laika (b), 8. Barack Obama (a).

Communication Revolution: From Rotary Phones to Cell Phones

Question 1: When was the first rotary dial telephone introduced?
a) 1891
b) 1904
c) 1919
d) 1923

Question 2: What invention, introduced in 1876, marked the beginning of modern communication technology?
a) Telegraph
b) Telephone
c) Radio
d) Phonograph

Question 3: What communication service, introduced in 1973, allowed people to send messages electronically?
a) Fax machine
b) Email
c) Pagers
d) Telex

Question 4: Which company introduced the first commercially available mobile phone in 1983?
a) Nokia
b) Motorola
c) AT&T
d) Ericsson

Question 5: What 1990s innovation made text messaging possible?
a) Short Message Service (SMS)
b) Wireless Application Protocol (WAP)
c) Global Positioning System (GPS)
d) Voice over Internet Protocol (VoIP)

Question 6: What type of phone became iconic for its folding design in the early 2000s?
a) Motorola Razr
b) Nokia 3310
c) BlackBerry
d) Siemens SL45

Question 7: When was the first iPhone introduced, marking a significant leap in mobile communication?
a) 2004
b) 2005
c) 2007
d) 2009

Question 8: What communication app, launched in 2009, revolutionized global text and video messaging?
a) WhatsApp
b) Skype
c) Viber
d) Facebook Messenger

Answers: The correct answers are: 1. 1891 (a), 2. Telephone (b), 3. Email (b), 4. Motorola (b), 5. Short Message Service (SMS) (a), 6. Motorola Razr (a), 7. 2007 (c), 8. WhatsApp (a).

The Internet Age Begins: Inventions That Shaped the 1990s

Question 1: What year was the World Wide Web made publicly available?
a) 1991
b) 1993
c) 1995
d) 1997

Question 2: What search engine, launched in 1998, became one of the most dominant tech companies?
a) Yahoo!
b) AltaVista
c) Google
d) Ask Jeeves

Question 3: What was the name of the first web browser, introduced in 1993?
a) Netscape Navigator
b) Mosaic
c) Internet Explorer
d) Opera

Question 4: What online retail giant, founded in 1994, began as a bookstore?
a) Amazon
b) eBay
c) Overstock
d) Walmart.com

Question 5: Which messaging service, launched in the 1990s, became iconic for its screen names and AIM chats?
a) ICQ
b) AOL Instant Messenger
c) MSN Messenger
d) Yahoo! Messenger

Question 6: What tech company released the first MP3 player, the MPMan, in 1998?
a) Sony
b) Apple
c) Diamond Multimedia
d) Saehan Information Systems

Question 7: What was the first popular blogging platform, launched in 1999?
a) WordPress
b) Blogger
c) LiveJournal
d) Xanga

Question 8: What file-sharing service, launched in 1999, revolutionized the music industry?
a) Napster
b) LimeWire
c) Kazaa
d) BitTorrent

Answers: The correct answers are: 1. 1991 (a), 2. Google (c), 3. Mosaic (b), 4. Amazon (a), 5. AOL Instant Messenger (b), 6. Saehan Information Systems (d), 7. Blogger (b), 8. Napster (a).

Disneyland Dreams: The Happiest Place on Earth Opens in 1955

Question 1: In what California city did Disneyland first open its gates in 1955?
a) Los Angeles
b) Anaheim
c) San Diego
d) San Francisco

Question 2: Who was the visionary behind the creation of Disneyland?
a) Walt Disney
b) Roy Disney
c) Carl Laemmle
d) John Lasseter

Question 3: What was the first themed land visitors entered upon entering Disneyland?
a) Tomorrowland
b) Main Street, U.S.A.
c) Adventureland
d) Fantasyland

Question 4: Which ride was among the original attractions when Disneyland opened?
a) Pirates of the Caribbean
b) Jungle Cruise
c) Space Mountain
d) Haunted Mansion

Question 5: What year did Disneyland celebrate its 10th anniversary, also known as the "Tencennial"?
a) 1963
b) 1965
c) 1967
d) 1970

Question 6: What iconic castle is the centerpiece of Disneyland?
a) Cinderella Castle
b) Sleeping Beauty Castle
c) Snow White Castle
d) Aurora Castle

Question 7: Which Disneyland ride, inspired by international cultures, features the famous song "It's a Small World"?
a) The Enchanted Tiki Room
b) Small World Adventure
c) It's a Small World
d) Global Carousel

Question 8: Which Disney park became the second to open after Disneyland, launching in 1971?
a) Disney California Adventure
b) Tokyo Disneyland
c) Walt Disney World
d) Disneyland Paris

Answers: The correct answers are: 1. Anaheim (b), 2. Walt Disney (a), 3. Main Street, U.S.A. (b), 4. Jungle Cruise (b), 5. 1965 (b), 6. Sleeping Beauty Castle (b), 7. It's a Small World (c), 8. Walt Disney World (c).

British Invasion: When the UK Took Over the Charts

Question 1: What iconic British band is credited with launching the British Invasion in the United States?
a) The Rolling Stones
b) The Who
c) The Beatles
d) The Kinks

Question 2: Which Beatles song was their first #1 hit in the U.S?
a) "I Want to Hold Your Hand"
b) "She Loves You"
c) "Love Me Do"
d) "Can't Buy Me Love"

Question 3: Which British band, known for their hit "(I Can't Get No) Satisfaction," became a major rival to The Beatles?
a) The Animals
b) The Rolling Stones
c) The Dave Clark Five
d) Herman's Hermits

Question 4: What iconic British rock guitarist founded The Yardbirds and later Cream?
a) Eric Clapton
b) Pete Townshend
c) Jimmy Page
d) Keith Richards

Question 5: Which British pop star, known as the "British Elvis," gained international fame in the 1960s?
a) Cliff Richard
b) Dusty Springfield
c) Tom Jones
d) Gerry Marsden

Question 6: What 1960s festival, featuring many British bands, symbolized the height of the counterculture movement?
a) Isle of Wight Festival
b) Woodstock
c) Monterey Pop Festival
d) Glastonbury

Question 7: Which British band popularized the rock opera genre with *Tommy* in 1969?
a) The Kinks
b) The Who
c) Pink Floyd
d) Genesis

Question 8: What British female artist was known for hits like "You Don't Have to Say You Love Me" during the British Invasion?
a) Petula Clark
b) Lulu
c) Dusty Springfield
d) Sandie Shaw

Answers: The correct answers are: 1. The Beatles (c), 2. "I Want to Hold Your Hand" (a), 3. The Rolling Stones (b), 4. Eric Clapton (a), 5. Cliff Richard (a), 6. Isle of Wight Festival (a), 7. The Who (b), 8. Dusty Springfield (c).

Plastic Fantastic: The Rise of Synthetic Materials

Question 1: Which synthetic fiber, introduced by DuPont in 1935, became widely used in clothing?
a) Polyester
b) Nylon
c) Rayon
d) Spandex

Question 2: What plastic, invented in the 1900s, became known as "the material of a thousand uses"?
a) Bakelite
b) Polypropylene
c) PVC
d) Teflon

Question 3: What popular 1950s Tupperware product revolutionized food storage?
a) Snap-on lids
b) Plastic containers
c) Reusable baggies
d) Seal-tight bowls

Question 4: Which material, introduced in the 1940s, became the standard for nonstick cookware?
a) Bakelite
b) Teflon
c) Silicone
d) Polyurethane

Question 5: What decade saw the invention of polyester as a widely used fabric?
a) 1940s
b) 1950s
c) 1960s
d) 1970s

Question 6: What popular toy, introduced in 1959, was made almost entirely of plastic?
a) LEGO bricks
b) Barbie
c) Play-Doh
d) Hula Hoop

Question 7: What lightweight material, introduced in the 1950s, became essential for packaging?
a) Styrofoam
b) Polypropylene
c) Cellophane
d) Polyethylene

Question 8: What environmental issue in the 1980s raised concerns about the widespread use of plastics?
a) Acid rain
b) Ozone depletion
c) Plastic pollution in oceans
d) Landfill overflow

Answers: The correct answers are: 1. Nylon (b), 2. Bakelite (a), 3. Plastic containers (b), 4. Teflon (b), 5. 1950s (b), 6. Barbie (b), 7. Styrofoam (a), 8. Plastic pollution in oceans (c).

Cultural Shifts: Music, Art, and Fashion of the Counterculture

Question 1: What 1969 event became a defining moment of the counterculture movement?
a) Monterey Pop Festival
b) Altamont Free Concert
c) Woodstock
d) Isle of Wight Festival

Question 2: Which iconic rock band released *Sgt. Pepper's Lonely Hearts Club Band* in 1967, marking a shift in music?
a) The Rolling Stones
b) The Beatles
c) Pink Floyd
d) The Grateful Dead

Question 3: What psychedelic artist is best known for creating vibrant concert posters in the 1960s?
a) Andy Warhol
b) Peter Max
c) Wes Wilson
d) Roy Lichtenstein

Question 4: What term described the bold, experimental art and music emerging in San Francisco during the 1960s?
a) Beat Movement
b) Psychedelic Movement
c) Surrealist Wave
d) Dadaism

Question 5: Which fashion item, associated with the hippie movement, became a symbol of peace and rebellion?
a) Bell-bottom jeans
b) Tie-dye shirts
c) Beaded necklaces
d) Leather fringe jackets

Question 6: What legendary guitarist performed a memorable rendition of "The Star-Spangled Banner" at Woodstock?
a) Jimi Hendrix
b) Eric Clapton
c) Pete Townshend
d) Carlos Santana

Question 7: What magazine, founded in 1967, chronicled the counterculture's music, art, and politics?
a) *Life*
b) *Rolling Stone*
c) *Time*
d) *Newsweek*

Question 8: What art technique, popularized by Andy Warhol, blended consumer culture with fine art?
a) Cubism
b) Abstract Expressionism
c) Pop Art
d) Minimalism

Answers: The correct answers are: 1. Woodstock (c), 2. The Beatles (b), 3. Wes Wilson (c), 4. Psychedelic Movement (b), 5. Tie-dye shirts (b), 6. Jimi Hendrix (a), 7. *Rolling Stone* (b), 8. Pop Art (c).

From Volkswagen to Apple: Game-Changing Print Ads

Question 1: What iconic Volkswagen ad from the 1960s featured the tagline "Think Small"?
a) Beetle
b) Kombi Van
c) Passat
d) Golf

Question 2: Which brand's print ad in 1984 launched the Macintosh computer with the tagline "Why 1984 won't be like 1984"?
a) IBM
b) Apple
c) Microsoft
d) Hewlett-Packard

Question 3: What print ad from the 1970s famously depicted a Native American shedding a tear about pollution?
a) Keep America Beautiful
b) Sierra Club
c) Greenpeace
d) Earth Day

Question 4: What brand created the groundbreaking campaign "We try harder" in the 1960s?
a) Hertz
b) Avis
c) Enterprise
d) National Car Rental

Question 5: Which car brand used the phrase "It's not your father's Oldsmobile" in its 1980s ads?
a) Buick
b) Chevrolet
c) Oldsmobile
d) Chrysler

Question 6: What cosmetics company made history with its slogan "Because you're worth it" in the 1970s?
a) Estée Lauder
b) Maybelline
c) L'Oréal
d) Revlon

Question 7: What print ad campaign, launched in the 1980s, encouraged milk consumption with the tagline "Got Milk?"
a) National Dairy Association
b) American Dairy Farmers
c) California Milk Processor Board
d) Dairy Farmers of America

Question 8: Which sneaker brand created the legendary "Just Do It" campaign in 1988?
a) Adidas
b) Nike
c) Reebok
d) Puma

Answers: The correct answers are: 1. Beetle (a), 2. Apple (b), 3. Keep America Beautiful (a), 4. Avis (b), 5. Oldsmobile (c), 6. L'Oréal (c), 7. California Milk Processor Board (c), 8. Nike (b).

Home Run Heroes: Baseball Legends of the Baby Boomer Era

Question 1: Which player broke Babe Ruth's home run record in 1974?
a) Willie Mays
b) Hank Aaron
c) Reggie Jackson
d) Mickey Mantle

Question 2: Who was the first African American player in Major League Baseball?
a) Jackie Robinson
b) Satchel Paige
c) Larry Doby
d) Roy Campanella

Question 3: What New York Yankees player was known as "The Mick"?
a) Joe DiMaggio
b) Lou Gehrig
c) Mickey Mantle
d) Yogi Berra

Question 4: What player hit a record 61 home runs in 1961?
a) Hank Aaron
b) Roger Maris
c) Ted Williams
d) Frank Robinson

Question 5: Which player, known as "Mr. October," was famous for his postseason heroics?
a) Pete Rose
b) Reggie Jackson
c) Carlton Fisk
d) Johnny Bench

Question 6: What team won the most World Series titles during the 1950s?
a) New York Yankees
b) Brooklyn Dodgers
c) St. Louis Cardinals
d) Boston Red Sox

Question 7: What pitcher holds the record for the most career strikeouts in MLB history?
a) Nolan Ryan
b) Sandy Koufax
c) Tom Seaver
d) Randy Johnson

Question 8: Who was the first designated hitter to be inducted into the Baseball Hall of Fame?
a) Edgar Martinez
b) David Ortiz
c) Paul Molitor
d) Frank Thomas

Answers: The correct answers are: 1. Hank Aaron (b), 2. Jackie Robinson (a), 3. Mickey Mantle (c), 4. Roger Maris (b), 5. Reggie Jackson (b), 6. New York Yankees (a), 7. Nolan Ryan (a), 8. Edgar Martinez (a).

You're the Bees Knees: Slang Words That Stuck Around

Question 1: What 1950s slang term refers to a cool and confident person?
a) Hepcat
b) Greaser
c) Beatnik
d) Square

Question 2: What 1960s slang term meant "great" or "cool"?
a) Far out
b) Groovy
c) Boss
d) Fab

Question 3: Which slang term, popular in the 1980s, described someone who was preppy or trendy?
a) Yuppie
b) Rad
c) Gnarly
d) Tubular

Question 4: What term, originating in the 1940s, was used to describe someone very attractive?
a) Dreamboat
b) Fox
c) Doll
d) Babe

Question 5: What phrase, popular in the 1970s, meant to relax or calm down?
a) Cool it
b) Lay low
c) Chill out
d) Take a breather

Question 6: What 1990s phrase became synonymous with sarcasm or irony?
a) Whatever
b) Yeah, right
c) As if
d) Totally

Question 7: Which term from the 1950s referred to an out-of-touch or boring person?
a) Nerd
b) Dweeb
c) Square
d) Drag

Question 8: What term, used throughout the Baby Boomer era, refers to someone who is wealthy or extravagant?
a) Loaded
b) Fat cat
c) Big shot
d) High roller

Answers: The correct answers are: 1. Hepcat (a), 2. Groovy (b), 3. Yuppie (a), 4. Dreamboat (a), 5. Cool it (a), 6. Yeah, right (b), 7. Square (c), 8. Loaded (a).

Leading Ladies and Hollywood Hunks: Stars Across the Decades

Question 1: Which actress starred in the 1953 film *Roman Holiday*, earning an Academy Award for Best Actress?
a) Audrey Hepburn
b) Grace Kelly
c) Elizabeth Taylor
d) Marilyn Monroe

Question 2: What leading man was known as "The King of Hollywood" during the Golden Age of Cinema?
a) Clark Gable
b) Cary Grant
c) James Stewart
d) Humphrey Bogart

Question 3: Which actress became a 1960s icon for her role in *Breakfast at Tiffany's*?
a) Audrey Hepburn
b) Sophia Loren
c) Julie Andrews
d) Natalie Wood

Question 4: What Hollywood hunk starred in the 1967 film *The Graduate*, propelling him to fame?
a) Dustin Hoffman
b) Robert Redford
c) Paul Newman
d) Warren Beatty

Question 5: Which actress won an Academy Award for her role in *Terms of Endearment* in 1983?
a) Meryl Streep
b) Jessica Lange
c) Shirley MacLaine
d) Jane Fonda

Question 6: Which actor played Indiana Jones in the *Raiders of the Lost Ark* series?
a) Tom Selleck
b) Harrison Ford
c) Kurt Russell
d) Kevin Costner

Question 7: What actress, known for her comedic roles, starred in *When Harry Met Sally* in 1989?
a) Meg Ryan
b) Diane Keaton
c) Sally Field
d) Goldie Hawn

Question 8: Who starred as the titular character in the 1997 film *Titanic*, cementing his status as a Hollywood heartthrob?
a) Brad Pitt
b) Tom Cruise
c) Leonardo DiCaprio
d) Matt Damon

Answers: The correct answers are: 1. Audrey Hepburn (a), 2. Clark Gable (a), 3. Audrey Hepburn (a), 4. Dustin Hoffman (a), 5. Shirley MacLaine (c), 6. Harrison Ford (b), 7. Meg Ryan (a), 8. Leonardo DiCaprio (c).

The Eisenhower Era: Politics and Prosperity in the 1950s

Question 1: Who was the U.S. president during most of the 1950s?
a) Harry S. Truman
b) Dwight D. Eisenhower
c) John F. Kennedy
d) Richard Nixon

Question 2: What major interstate system was established under Eisenhower in 1956?
a) The Federal Highway System
b) The Eisenhower Interstate System
c) The National Roadways Initiative
d) The U.S. Route Network

Question 3: What Cold War alliance, formed in 1949, included the U.S. and Western European countries?
a) NATO
b) SEATO
c) Warsaw Pact
d) The League of Nations

Question 4: What landmark Supreme Court case in 1954 declared racial segregation in public schools unconstitutional?
a) Brown v. Board of Education
b) Roe v. Wade
c) Plessy v. Ferguson
d) Miranda v. Arizona

Question 5: What global event in 1957 involved the launch of the first artificial satellite?
a) Apollo 1
b) Sputnik
c) Explorer 1
d) Telstar

Question 6: What term was used to describe the fear of communist influence during the 1950s?
a) The Red Scare
b) The Domino Effect
c) McCarthyism
d) The Iron Curtain

Question 7: What economic phenomenon of the 1950s saw a rise in consumerism and suburban living?
a) The Industrial Boom
b) The Consumer Revolution
c) The Suburban Shift
d) The Post-War Boom

Question 8: What program allowed World War II veterans to buy homes and attend college?
a) The New Deal
b) The Marshall Plan
c) The G.I. Bill
d) The Fair Housing Act

Answers: The correct answers are: 1. Dwight D. Eisenhower (b), 2. The Federal Highway System (a), 3. NATO (a), 4. Brown v. Board of Education (a), 5. Sputnik (b), 6. McCarthyism (c), 7. The Post-War Boom (d), 8. The G.I. Bill (c).

The National Parks Boom: Nature's Wonders in the Baby Boomer Era

Question 1: Which U.S. president signed the Wilderness Act into law in 1964, protecting federal land?
a) John F. Kennedy
b) Lyndon B. Johnson
c) Richard Nixon
d) Jimmy Carter

Question 2: What iconic canyon, located in Arizona, became one of the most-visited national parks in the 1950s?
a) Grand Canyon
b) Bryce Canyon
c) Zion Canyon
d) Antelope Canyon

Question 3: What California national park is home to Half Dome and El Capitan?
a) Yosemite
b) Sequoia
c) Kings Canyon
d) Joshua Tree

Question 4: What environmentalist is credited with helping establish many national parks and co-founding the Sierra Club?
a) John Muir
b) Rachel Carson
c) Aldo Leopold
d) Gifford Pinchot

Question 5: What national park, located in Wyoming, is famous for its geothermal geysers like Old Faithful?
a) Yellowstone
b) Grand Teton
c) Glacier
d) Crater Lake

Question 6: What was the name of the program launched in the 1960s to improve park facilities and accessibility?
a) Mission 66
b) Project Parks
c) Park Renewal Initiative
d) Nature's Legacy

Question 7: What coastal national park in Florida is known for its diverse ecosystem and alligators?
a) Everglades
b) Biscayne
c) Dry Tortugas
d) Big Cypress

Question 8: What decade saw the largest expansion of the National Park Service?
a) 1930s
b) 1940s
c) 1950s
d) 1960s

Answers: The correct answers are:
1. Lyndon B. Johnson (b), 2. Grand Canyon (a), 3. Yosemite (a), 4. John Muir (a), 5. Yellowstone (a), 6. Mission 66 (a), 7. Everglades (a), 8. 1960s (d).

Sock Hops and Soda Shops: Everyday Talk of the 1950s Teen Scene

Question 1: What was a "sock hop" in the 1950s?
a) A dance held in a school gymnasium
b) A shoe store sale
c) A new fashion trend
d) A style of swing dancing

Question 2: What was a popular drink served at soda fountains in the 1950s?
a) Cola float
b) Malted milkshake
c) Root beer spritzer
d) Cherry limeade

Question 3: What slang term did teens use in the 1950s to describe a good friend?
a) Ace
b) Cool cat
c) Buddy
d) Pal

Question 4: What term referred to a stylish and confident young man?
a) Hepcat
b) Greaser
c) Jock
d) Dreamboat

Question 5: What activity did 1950s teens often do while hanging out at soda shops?
a) Playing pinball
b) Watching TV
c) Reading comics
d) Listening to live bands

Question 6: What 1950s car feature became a symbol of teen rebellion and freedom?
a) Convertible tops
b) Whitewall tires
c) Tailfins
d) Chrome bumpers

Question 7: What was a "bobby-soxer"?
a) A young girl wearing ankle socks
b) A soda shop waitress
c) A new dance craze
d) A type of shoe popular in the 1950s

Question 8: What term described a dance move popular in the 1950s?
a) The Twist
b) The Jitterbug
c) The Mash
d) The Lindy Hop

Answers: The correct answers are: 1. A dance held in a school gymnasium (a), 2. Malted milkshake (b), 3. Buddy (c), 4. Greaser (b), 5. Playing pinball (a), 6. Convertible tops (a), 7. A young girl wearing ankle socks (a), 8. The Jitterbug (b).

From Tupperware to TVs: Household Staples of the '50s and '60s

Question 1: What brand introduced airtight plastic food storage containers in the 1950s?
a) Rubbermaid
b) Pyrex
c) Tupperware
d) KitchenAid

Question 2: What household appliance became widespread in American homes during the 1950s?
a) Dishwasher
b) Microwave oven
c) Washing machine
d) Television

Question 3: What cleaning tool, first sold in 1954, used a disposable paper bag?
a) Vacuum cleaner
b) Dustbuster
c) Floor polisher
d) Carpet shampooer

Question 4: Which 1960s kitchen appliance promised "set it and forget it" convenience?
a) Slow cooker
b) Electric blender
c) Toaster oven
d) Stand mixer

Question 5: What furniture item, introduced in the 1960s, became a symbol of modern design?
a) Bean bag chair
b) Recliner
c) Eames lounge chair
d) Foldable TV tray

Question 6: What innovation in the 1950s allowed families to watch pre-recorded TV shows?
a) VCR
b) Color television
c) Videotape recorder
d) Cable television

Question 7: What type of dinnerware became popular for its lightweight durability in the 1950s?
a) Ceramic plates
b) Plastic plates
c) Melamine dinnerware
d) Stainless steel trays

Question 8: Which company popularized the concept of frozen TV dinners in the 1950s?
a) Swanson
b) Banquet
c) Stouffer's
d) Hungry-Man

Answers: The correct answers are: 1. Tupperware (c), 2. Television (d), 3. Vacuum cleaner (a), 4. Slow cooker (a), 5. Eames lounge chair (c), 6. Videotape recorder (c), 7. Melamine dinnerware (c), 8. Swanson (a).

Racing Legends: From NASCAR to the Indy 500

Question 1: Who was the first driver to win four Indianapolis 500 races?
a) A.J. Foyt
b) Mario Andretti
c) Rick Mears
d) Al Unser

Question 2: What year was NASCAR officially founded?
a) 1939
b) 1948
c) 1953
d) 1960

Question 3: Which car manufacturer dominated the NASCAR circuit in the 1950s?
a) Chevrolet
b) Ford
c) Plymouth
d) Oldsmobile

Question 4: Who was known as "The King" of NASCAR for his record seven championships?
a) Richard Petty
b) Dale Earnhardt
c) Jeff Gordon
d) Cale Yarborough

Question 5: Which IndyCar driver famously won the Triple Crown of Motorsport?
a) Jackie Stewart
b) Mario Andretti
c) Graham Hill
d) Emerson Fittipaldi

Question 6: What track is known as the birthplace of NASCAR?
a) Daytona International Speedway
b) Talladega Superspeedway
c) Charlotte Motor Speedway
d) Darlington Raceway

Question 7: What racing innovation was introduced at the Indy 500 in 1965?
a) Rear-engine cars
b) Turbocharged engines
c) Slick tires
d) Pit stop refueling

Question 8: What car number was most associated with Richard Petty during his career?
a) 3
b) 24
c) 43
d) 88

Answers: The correct answers are: 1. A.J. Foyt (a), 2. 1948 (b), 3. Oldsmobile (d), 4. Richard Petty (a), 5. Graham Hill (c), 6. Daytona International Speedway (a), 7. Rear-engine cars (a), 8. 43 (c).

Remote Control Favorites: 1980s and '90s TV Hits

Question 1: What 1980s sitcom followed the lives of the Huxtable family in Brooklyn?
a) *Family Ties*
b) *The Cosby Show*
c) *Growing Pains*
d) *Full House*

Question 2: Which teen drama debuted in 1990 and centered on a group of friends in Beverly Hills?
a) *Saved by the Bell*
b) *Dawson's Creek*
c) *Beverly Hills, 90210*
d) *Party of Five*

Question 3: What 1989 animated series featured a dysfunctional family from Springfield?
a) *The Flintstones*
b) *The Jetsons*
c) *The Simpsons*
d) *South Park*

Question 4: Which 1990s sitcom featured four women living in Miami, including Blanche and Dorothy?
a) *Designing Women*
b) *The Golden Girls*
c) *Living Single*
d) *Cheers*

Question 5: What show, hosted by Bob Saget, highlighted humorous home videos starting in 1989?
a) *America's Funniest Home Videos*
b) *Funniest People in America*
c) *Candid Camera*
d) *Home Video Highlights*

Question 6: Which 1980s action series starred David Hasselhoff and his talking car, KITT?
a) *Magnum P.I.*
b) *Knight Rider*
c) *The A-Team*
d) *MacGyver*

Question 7: What 1990s show featured six friends hanging out at Central Perk in New York City?
a) *Seinfeld*
b) *Friends*
c) *Will & Grace*
d) *Mad About You*

Question 8: Which sci-fi series, debuting in 1987, continued the adventures of the USS Enterprise?
a) *Star Trek: The Original Series*
b) *Star Trek: Voyager*
c) *Star Trek: Deep Space Nine*
d) *Star Trek: The Next Generation*

Answers: The correct answers are: 1. *The Cosby Show* (b), 2. *Beverly Hills, 90210* (c), 3. *The Simpsons* (c), 4. *The Golden Girls* (b), 5. *America's Funniest Home Videos* (a), 6. *Knight Rider* (b), 7. *Friends* (b), 8. *Star Trek: The Next Generation* (d).

The Evolution of Fast Food Ads: Burgers, Fries, and Mascots

Question 1: Which fast-food chain used the slogan "Where's the beef?" in the 1980s?
a) McDonald's
b) Wendy's
c) Burger King
d) Arby's

Question 2: What iconic clown character has been McDonald's mascot since the 1960s?
a) Ronald McDonald
b) The Burger King
c) The Hamburglar
d) Grimace

Question 3: Which fast-food chain introduced the "Have it your way" slogan in the 1970s?
a) McDonald's
b) Wendy's
c) Burger King
d) Hardee's

Question 4: What fast-food chain launched its iconic "Eat Mor Chikin" campaign featuring cows in 1995?
a) Chick-fil-A
b) KFC
c) Popeyes
d) Raising Cane's

Question 5: Which mascot, introduced in the 1980s, represented Taco Bell and became a cultural phenomenon?
a) Taco Chihuahua
b) Taco Pete
c) Nacho the Cat
d) The Bell Beefer

Question 6: What fast-food company used the jingle "You deserve a break today" in the 1970s?
a) McDonald's
b) Burger King
c) Subway
d) Dairy Queen

Question 7: Which fast-food restaurant's ads featured the "Five-dollar footlong" jingle in the 2000s?
a) Subway
b) Quiznos
c) Jimmy John's
d) Firehouse Subs

Question 8: Which burger chain is known for its square patties and Frosty dessert?
a) McDonald's
b) Burger King
c) Wendy's
d) White Castle

Answers: The correct answers are: 1. Wendy's (b), 2. Ronald McDonald (a), 3. Burger King (c), 4. Chick-fil-A (a), 5. Taco Chihuahua (a), 6. McDonald's (a), 7. Subway (a), 8. Wendy's (c).

Drive-Ins and Diners: Classic American Eats on the Go

Question 1: What food item, often paired with root beer, became a staple at drive-ins?
a) Hamburger
b) Hot dog
c) Corn dog
d) French fries

Question 2: Which 1950s drive-in restaurant chain is famous for its carhops on roller skates?
a) A&W
b) Sonic Drive-In
c) Steak 'n Shake
d) Dairy Queen

Question 3: What milkshake flavor became synonymous with the 1950s diner experience?
a) Vanilla
b) Chocolate
c) Strawberry
d) Mint

Question 4: What iconic American dish, served at diners, consists of sliced beef, gravy, and bread?
a) Salisbury steak
b) Meatloaf
c) Chipped beef on toast
d) Roast beef sandwich

Question 5: Which dessert, served in aluminum tins, was a diner favorite in the 1950s?
a) Apple pie
b) Banana split
c) Chocolate cream pie
d) Icebox cake

Question 6: What drink, served at soda fountains, combined carbonated water with flavored syrup?
a) Egg cream
b) Ice cream soda
c) Cherry cola
d) Phosphate

Question 7: What breakfast item, popularized in diners, is made from shredded potatoes and pan-fried?
a) Hash browns
b) Home fries
c) Potato pancakes
d) Tater tots

Question 8: What drive-in chain, founded in California in the 1940s, introduced the first two-way speaker system for ordering?
a) In-N-Out Burger
b) Sonic Drive-In
c) A&W
d) White Castle

Answers: The correct answers are: 1. Hamburger (a), 2. Sonic Drive-In (b), 3. Strawberry (c), 4. Chipped beef on toast (c), 5. Chocolate cream pie (c), 6. Phosphate (d), 7. Hash browns (a), 8. In-N-Out Burger (a).

Disco Dazzle: Bell-Bottoms, Jumpsuits, and the Glitter of the 1970s

Question 1: What fabric, often associated with disco fashion, was prized for its shine and stretch?
a) Spandex
b) Polyester
c) Nylon
d) Velvet

Question 2: Which unisex garment became a staple of 1970s disco wear?
a) Jumpsuit
b) Bell-bottoms
c) Tracksuit
d) Miniskirt

Question 3: What accessory, often glittery or metallic, was a must-have for 1970s disco dancers?
a) Platform shoes
b) Leather gloves
c) Aviator sunglasses
d) Headbands

Question 4: What famous New York City nightclub became the epicenter of disco culture?
a) The Roxy
b) CBGB
c) Studio 54
d) The Cotton Club

Question 5: Which disco anthem by Gloria Gaynor became an empowering anthem of the decade?
a) "Last Dance"
b) "Stayin' Alive"
c) "I Will Survive"
d) "Funkytown"

Question 6: What hairstyle, often voluminous and natural, was popular in the disco era?
a) The Afro
b) The Shag
c) The Mullet
d) Feathered hair

Question 7: Which 1977 movie, starring John Travolta, helped bring disco fashion into the mainstream?
a) *Saturday Night Fever*
b) *Grease*
c) *Footloose*
d) *Dirty Dancing*

Question 8: What disco group was known for their iconic hit "Le Freak"?
a) Bee Gees
b) Chic
c) Village People
d) ABBA

Answers: The correct answers are: 1. Polyester (b), 2. Jumpsuit (a), 3. Platform shoes (a), 4. Studio 54 (c), 5. "I Will Survive" (c), 6. The Afro (a), 7. *Saturday Night Fever* (a), 8. Chic (b).

Outdoor Adventures: Bikes, Roller Skates, and Backyard Fun

Question 1: What iconic bike, introduced in the 1960s, featured high-rise handlebars and a banana seat?
a) Schwinn Sting-Ray
b) Raleigh Chopper
c) BMX
d) Huffy Cruiser

Question 2: What 1970s roller skate innovation allowed for greater control and speed?
a) Plastic wheels
b) Rubber stoppers
c) Adjustable straps
d) Ball bearings

Question 3: What backyard activity involved jumping on a large elastic surface?
a) Pogo stick
b) Trampoline
c) Slip 'n Slide
d) Lawn darts

Question 4: Which outdoor toy, invented in 1969, used water to create a slick surface for sliding?
a) Sprinkler pad
b) Water slide
c) Slip 'n Slide
d) Splash mat

Question 5: What was the popular name for the two-wheeled scooter that gained popularity in the 1990s?
a) Razor scooter
b) Kick scooter
c) Power scooter
d) Street scooter

Question 6: What iconic outdoor toy used a string and two sticks to keep a disk spinning?
a) Yo-yo
b) Diabolo
c) Hula hoop
d) Frisbee

Question 7: Which classic backyard game involved tossing small, weighted bags into a hole on a slanted board?
a) Horseshoes
b) Cornhole
c) Bocce
d) Croquet

Question 8: What outdoor game, popular in the 1970s and later banned due to safety concerns, involved throwing pointed projectiles?
a) Lawn darts
b) Horseshoes
c) Ring toss
d) Bocce

Answers: The correct answers are: 1. Schwinn Sting-Ray (a), 2. Ball bearings (d), 3. Trampoline (b), 4. Slip 'n Slide (c), 5. Razor scooter (a), 6. Diabolo (b), 7. Cornhole (b), 8. Lawn darts (a).

Far Out and Groovy: Slang of the 1960s Counterculture

Question 1: What 1960s slang term meant something was excellent or great?
a) Groovy
b) Boss
c) Swell
d) Solid

Question 2: What term, popular among hippies, referred to a deeply spiritual or eye-opening experience?
a) Cosmic
b) Heavy
c) Mind-blowing
d) Outta sight

Question 3: What 1960s slang word was used to describe someone who was out of touch or uncool?
a) Drag
b) Square
c) Beat
d) Jive

Question 4: What phrase was used by hippies to express love and peace?
a) Love beads
b) Peace and love
c) Make love, not war
d) Good vibes

Question 5: What term, often used in the counterculture, referred to a police officer?
a) Pig
b) Fuzz
c) Cop
d) Heat

Question 6: What phrase, popularized by Timothy Leary, encouraged people to explore altered states of consciousness?
a) Turn on, tune in, drop out
b) Expand your mind
c) Reach for the stars
d) Explore and evolve

Question 7: Which word was used to describe someone who was incredibly relaxed or laid-back?
a) Chill
b) Cool
c) Mellow
d) Zen

Question 8: What slang term referred to hitchhiking in the 1960s?
a) Catching a ride
b) Thumb a lift
c) Hitching
d) Road tripping

Answers: The correct answers are: 1. Groovy (a), 2. Mind-blowing (c), 3. Square (b), 4. Make love, not war (c), 5. Fuzz (b), 6. Turn on, tune in, drop out (a), 7. Mellow (c), 8. Thumb a lift (b).

Heart Transplants and Human Progress: Medical Milestones

Question 1: Who performed the world's first successful human heart transplant in 1967?
a) Dr. Christian Barnard
b) Dr. Denton Cooley
c) Dr. Michael DeBakey
d) Dr. Jonas Salk

Question 2: What medical imaging technique, introduced in the 1970s, revolutionized diagnostics?
a) MRI
b) Ultrasound
c) CT Scan
d) X-Ray

Question 3: Which vaccine, developed in the 1950s, effectively eradicated polio in most of the world?
a) Smallpox vaccine
b) Polio vaccine
c) Hepatitis vaccine
d) Measles vaccine

Question 4: In what year was the first test-tube baby born via in-vitro fertilization (IVF)?
a) 1968
b) 1978
c) 1988
d) 1998

Question 5: What 1980s breakthrough medication significantly improved the treatment of HIV/AIDS?
a) AZT
b) Penicillin
c) Insulin
d) Statins

Question 6: What surgical technique, developed in the 1980s, allows for minimally invasive procedures?
a) Arthroscopy
b) Laparoscopy
c) Open-heart surgery
d) Microsurgery

Question 7: What organ was first successfully transplanted in humans in 1954?
a) Kidney
b) Liver
c) Lung
d) Heart

Question 8: What genetic editing tool, introduced in the 2010s, marked a major advance in medicine?
a) CRISPR
b) PCR
c) DNA Sequencing
d) Gene Splicing

Answers: The correct answers are: 1. Dr. Christian Barnard (a), 2. CT Scan (c), 3. Polio vaccine (b), 4. 1978 (b), 5. AZT (a), 6. Laparoscopy (b), 7. Kidney (a), 8. CRISPR (a).

Chart-Topping Duos and Groups: Harmony Through the Years

Question 1: What sibling duo was known for hits like "Close to You" in the 1970s?
a) The Everly Brothers
b) The Carpenters
c) Sonny and Cher
d) Simon & Garfunkel

Question 2: Which British band became the face of the 1960s British Invasion with songs like "Hey Jude"?
a) The Rolling Stones
b) The Beatles
c) The Who
d) The Kinks

Question 3: What 1980s duo sang the hit "Wake Me Up Before You Go-Go"?
a) Hall & Oates
b) Wham!
c) Tears for Fears
d) Pet Shop Boys

Question 4: Which 1970s group was famous for their disco hits like "Dancing Queen"?
a) ABBA
b) The Bee Gees
c) Chic
d) Sister Sledge

Question 5: What Motown group, led by Diana Ross, was known for hits like "Stop! In the Name of Love"?
a) The Supremes
b) The Temptations
c) The Four Tops
d) The Marvelettes

Question 6: Which 1990s boy band rose to fame with hits like "I Want It That Way"?
a) Backstreet Boys
b) NSYNC
c) Boyz II Men
d) New Kids on the Block

Question 7: What legendary 1980s duo had hits like "Rich Girl" and "Private Eyes"?
a) Eurythmics
b) Hall & Oates
c) Tears for Fears
d) Simon & Garfunkel

Question 8: What 1960s folk duo was famous for songs like "The Sound of Silence"?
a) Peter, Paul and Mary
b) Simon & Garfunkel
c) The Everly Brothers
d) The Kingston Trio

Answers: The correct answers are: 1. The Carpenters (b), 2. The Beatles (b), 3. Wham! (b), 4. ABBA (a), 5. The Supremes (a), 6. Backstreet Boys (a), 7. Hall & Oates (b), 8. Simon & Garfunkel (b).

Sports Milestones: Records, Streaks, and Unforgettable Moments

Question 1: Who was the first athlete to win seven gold medals in a single Olympic Games?
a) Michael Phelps
b) Mark Spitz
c) Carl Lewis
d) Jesse Owens

Question 2: What baseball player broke Lou Gehrig's record for consecutive games played in 1995?
a) Cal Ripken Jr.
b) Derek Jeter
c) Pete Rose
d) Hank Aaron

Question 3: Which NBA team had a record-breaking 72-win season in 1995-96?
a) Chicago Bulls
b) Los Angeles Lakers
c) Golden State Warriors
d) Boston Celtics

Question 4: What tennis player won the first four Grand Slam tournaments in a single year in 1938?
a) Rod Laver
b) Don Budge
c) Billie Jean King
d) Bjorn Borg

Question 5: What was the first country to win the FIFA World Cup in 1930?
a) Brazil
b) Germany
c) Uruguay
d) Argentina

Question 6: Who became the youngest heavyweight boxing champion in 1986?
a) Muhammad Ali
b) Mike Tyson
c) Evander Holyfield
d) George Foreman

Question 7: Which female gymnast scored the first perfect 10 in Olympic history?
a) Nadia Comaneci
b) Simone Biles
c) Olga Korbut
d) Mary Lou Retton

Question 8: Who is the only golfer to win all four major championships in the same calendar year?
a) Tiger Woods
b) Jack Nicklaus
c) Ben Hogan
d) Bobby Jones

Answers: The correct answers are: 1. Mark Spitz (b), 2. Cal Ripken Jr. (a), 3. Chicago Bulls (a), 4. Don Budge (b), 5. Uruguay (c), 6. Mike Tyson (b), 7. Nadia Comaneci (a), 8. Bobby Jones (d).

Collectibles Craze: Trading Cards, Stickers, and Happy Meal Toys

Question 1: What trading card series from 1952 is considered the most valuable among collectors?
a) Topps Baseball Cards
b) Fleer Basketball Cards
c) Upper Deck Cards
d) Bowman Football Cards

Question 2: What 1980s collectible featured cartoonishly grotesque characters in sticker form?
a) Garbage Pail Kids
b) Wacky Packages
c) Cabbage Patch Stickers
d) Mad Caps

Question 3: Which sports card company released the iconic Michael Jordan rookie card in 1986?
a) Topps
b) Fleer
c) Upper Deck
d) Panini

Question 4: What 1990s trading card game became a global phenomenon and included characters like Pikachu?
a) Yu-Gi-Oh!
b) Pokémon
c) Magic: The Gathering
d) Digimon

Question 5: Which McDonald's Happy Meal toy series from the 1990s became a collector's item?
a) Beanie Babies
b) Hot Wheels
c) Transformers
d) Furbys

Question 6: What trading card brand launched holographic cards in the 1990s?
a) Topps Stadium Club
b) Upper Deck
c) Fleer Ultra
d) Panini Prizm

Question 7: Which stickers, introduced in the 1970s, featured humorous parodies of consumer products?
a) Wacky Packages
b) Scratch n' Sniff
c) Garbage Pail Kids
d) Kool Kat Stickers

Question 8: What collectible toy, included in Kinder Surprise eggs, became a global sensation?
a) Smurfs
b) Miniature Cars
c) Kinder Minis
d) Toy Figurines

Answers: The correct answers are: 1. Topps Baseball Cards (a), 2. Garbage Pail Kids (a), 3. Fleer (b), 4. Pokémon (b), 5. Beanie Babies (a), 6. Upper Deck (b), 7. Wacky Packages (a), 8. Toy Figurines (d).

Saturday Night Fever: Disco and Dance Crazes of the 1970s

Question 1: What was the name of the dance style characterized by synchronized arm and leg movements to disco music?
a) The Hustle
b) The Bump
c) The Electric Slide
d) The Funky Chicken

Question 2: Which 1977 movie, starring John Travolta, helped make disco music and culture mainstream?
a) *Saturday Night Fever*
b) *Grease*
c) *Footloose*
d) *Urban Cowboy*

Question 3: What New York nightclub was the epicenter of disco culture in the late 1970s?
a) CBGB
b) Studio 54
c) The Roxy
d) The Palladium

Question 4: Which Bee Gees song, featured in *Saturday Night Fever*, became a disco anthem?
a) "Stayin' Alive"
b) "How Deep Is Your Love"
c) "Night Fever"
d) "You Should Be Dancing"

Question 5: What popular 1970s dance involved bumping hips with a partner?
a) The Bump
b) The Hustle
c) The Twist
d) The Robot

Question 6: Which instrument, often used in disco music, is known for its distinctive "wah-wah" sound?
a) Electric guitar
b) Synthesizer
c) Bass guitar
d) Clavinet

Question 7: Which female disco artist is known for hits like "Last Dance" and "Hot Stuff"?
a) Gloria Gaynor
b) Donna Summer
c) Diana Ross
d) Patti LaBelle

Question 8: What 1970s dance craze involved pointing fingers up and down in rhythm?
a) The Hustle
b) The YMCA
c) The Disco Finger
d) The Bus Stop

Muscle Cars and Power Rides: The Icons of the 1960s and 1970s

Question 1: What 1964 car is often credited with starting the muscle car era?
a) Ford Mustang
b) Pontiac GTO
c) Chevrolet Camaro
d) Dodge Charger

Question 2: Which muscle car was known as "The Judge"?
a) Plymouth Barracuda
b) Pontiac GTO
c) Dodge Challenger
d) Ford Torino

Question 3: What Dodge model became famous for its role in the TV show *The Dukes of Hazzard*?
a) Dodge Charger
b) Dodge Challenger
c) Dodge Dart
d) Dodge Super Bee

Question 4: What Chevy muscle car, introduced in 1967, was a direct competitor to the Ford Mustang?
a) Chevrolet Corvette
b) Chevrolet Camaro
c) Chevrolet Nova
d) Chevrolet Chevelle

Question 5: Which muscle car, introduced in 1970, featured the legendary HEMI engine?
a) Plymouth Superbird
b) Dodge Challenger
c) Chevrolet Chevelle SS
d) Ford Torino GT

Question 6: Which Ford model, introduced in 1964, became an iconic American sports car?
a) Ford Falcon
b) Ford Thunderbird
c) Ford Mustang
d) Ford Fairlane

Question 7: What feature, popular in muscle cars, was designed to reduce engine overheating?
a) Hood scoops
b) Turbochargers
c) Spoilers
d) Rear diffusers

Question 8: What nickname was given to high-performance Plymouth and Dodge cars of the late 1960s?
a) Super Bees
b) Road Runners
c) Mopar Muscle
d) Speed Demons

Answers: The correct answers are:
1. Pontiac GTO (b), 2. Pontiac GTO (b), 3. Dodge Charger (a), 4. Chevrolet Camaro (b), 5. Dodge Challenger (b), 6. Ford Mustang (c), 7. Hood scoops (a), 8. Mopar Muscle (c).

Mascot Mania: From Tony the Tiger to the Jolly Green Giant

Question 1: What cereal mascot is known for saying, "They're grrreat!"?
a) Toucan Sam
b) Tony the Tiger
c) Snap, Crackle, and Pop
d) The Trix Rabbit

Question 2: What mascot, introduced in the 1920s, represents Green Giant vegetables?
a) Sprout
b) Jolly Green Giant
c) Mr. Pea
d) Farmer Green

Question 3: Which advertising mascot is a cheerful sun wearing sunglasses, representing a breakfast juice?
a) Kool-Aid Man
b) Sunny D
c) Tropicana Sun
d) The Florida Orange Bird

Question 4: What fast-food mascot, introduced in the 1960s, is a clown known for his red hair?
a) Ronald McDonald
b) The Burger King
c) Colonel Sanders
d) Jack Box

Question 5: What Kool-Aid mascot is famous for crashing through walls and shouting, "Oh yeah!"?
a) Kool-Aid Kid
b) Kool-Aid Man
c) Kool Dude
d) The Red Jug

Question 6: What cereal mascot is a leprechaun who tries to keep his cereal away from kids?
a) Lucky the Leprechaun
b) Count Chocula
c) Toucan Sam
d) Sugar Bear

Question 7: What snack mascot is a smiling doughboy often poked in the stomach?
a) Pillsbury Doughboy
b) Michelin Man
c) Stay Puft Marshmallow Man
d) Mr. Poppin' Fresh

Question 8: Which animal mascot represents Cheetos and is known for his cool sunglasses?
a) Cool Cat
b) Tony the Tiger
c) Chester Cheetah
d) Felix the Cat

Answers: The correct answers are: 1. Tony the Tiger (b), 2. Jolly Green Giant (b), 3. The Florida Orange Bird (d), 4. Ronald McDonald (a), 5. Kool-Aid Man (b), 6. Lucky the Leprechaun (a), 7. Pillsbury Doughboy (a), 8. Chester Cheetah (c).

New Hollywood: The Directors Who Changed the Game in the '70s

Question 1: What director gained fame for *The Godfather* and *Apocalypse Now*?
a) George Lucas
b) Steven Spielberg
c) Francis Ford Coppola
d) Martin Scorsese

Question 2: Which director created *Star Wars* in 1977, forever changing science fiction?
a) Ridley Scott
b) Stanley Kubrick
c) George Lucas
d) James Cameron

Question 3: What Martin Scorsese film, released in 1976, starred Robert De Niro as a troubled taxi driver?
a) *Raging Bull*
b) *Taxi Driver*
c) *Mean Streets*
d) *The King of Comedy*

Question 4: What groundbreaking 1975 thriller made Steven Spielberg a household name?
a) *Jaws*
b) *Close Encounters of the Third Kind*
c) *E.T.*
d) *Poltergeist*

Question 5: Which director helmed the 1971 cult classic *A Clockwork Orange?*
a) Francis Ford Coppola
b) Stanley Kubrick
c) Brian De Palma
d) Peter Bogdanovich

Question 6: Which director's 1979 sci-fi horror film *Alien* became an instant classic?
a) Ridley Scott
b) James Cameron
c) John Carpenter
d) Stanley Kubrick

Question 7: What Robert Altman film, set in a mobile army hospital, became a hit in 1970?
a) *Patton*
b) *MASH**
c) *Catch-22*
d) *Apocalypse Now*

Question 8: Which director, known for *The Exorcist* in 1973, also directed *The French Connection?*
a) William Friedkin
b) Roman Polanski
c) Brian De Palma
d) John Frankenheimer

Bodacious and Rad: '80s Slang Words That Closed the Boomer Era

Question 1: What 1980s slang term meant something was excellent or amazing?
a) Awesome
b) Rad
c) Bodacious
d) Tubular

Question 2: What term referred to an attractive person during the 1980s?
a) Hottie
b) Fox
c) Babe
d) Dreamboat

Question 3: What phrase, popularized by Valley Girls, was used to express disbelief or sarcasm?
a) "As if!"
b) "Gag me with a spoon!"
c) "No way!"
d) "Whatever!"

Question 4: What slang word described a fashionable or trendy person in the 1980s?
a) Yuppie
b) Preppy
c) Trendy
d) Hipster

Question 5: What 1980s term referred to skipping school without permission?
a) Playing hooky
b) Ditching
c) Skipping
d) Cutting

Question 6: What word was used to describe a wild or crazy party in the 1980s?
a) Bash
b) Rager
c) Blowout
d) Shindig

Question 7: What was a common term for a nerdy or socially awkward person in the 1980s?
a) Geek
b) Square
c) Dork
d) Loser

Question 8: What was a slang term for a great-looking car or motorcycle in the 1980s?
a) Rad ride
b) Sweet wheels
c) Cool whip
d) Hot rod

Answers: The correct answers are: 1. Bodacious (c), 2. Fox (b), 3. "Gag me with a spoon!" (b), 4. Yuppie (a), 5. Ditching (b), 6. Rager (b), 7. Dork (c), 8. Hot rod (d).

Innovations on the Road: Seatbelts, Airbags, and Auto Advances

Question 1: In what year did Volvo introduce the three-point seatbelt, revolutionizing car safety?
a) 1955
b) 1959
c) 1962
d) 1967

Question 2: Which country was the first to require seatbelts in all passenger cars?
a) United States
b) Germany
c) Sweden
d) United Kingdom

Question 3: What car company introduced the first commercially available airbag in the 1970s?
a) General Motors
b) Chrysler
c) Mercedes-Benz
d) Ford

Question 4: What automotive innovation, introduced in the 1980s, significantly improved fuel efficiency?
a) Turbochargers
b) Catalytic converters
c) Anti-lock brakes
d) Fuel injection

Question 5: Which U.S. regulation in the 1960s required the installation of seatbelts in all new cars?
a) Highway Safety Act
b) National Traffic and Motor Vehicle Safety Act
c) Motor Vehicle Safety Act
d) Federal Safety Act

Question 6: What year saw the introduction of anti-lock braking systems (ABS) in consumer vehicles?
a) 1970
b) 1974
c) 1978
d) 1982

Question 7: What Japanese automaker was the first to mass-produce hybrid vehicles in the late 1990s?
a) Nissan
b) Honda
c) Toyota
d) Mitsubishi

Question 8: What car model became the first mass-market electric vehicle in the 2010s?
a) Nissan Leaf
b) Tesla Model S
c) Chevrolet Volt
d) Toyota Prius

Answers: The correct answers are: 1. 1959 (b), 2. Sweden (c), 3. General Motors (a), 4. Fuel injection (d), 5. National Traffic and Motor Vehicle Safety Act (b), 6. 1978 (c), 7. Toyota (c), 8. Nissan Leaf (a).

TV Dinners and Fast Food: The Rise of Convenience in the 1960s

Question 1: Which company is credited with popularizing TV dinners in the 1950s and 1960s?
a) Stouffer's
b) Swanson
c) Banquet
d) Marie Callender's

Question 2: What fast-food chain introduced the Filet-O-Fish sandwich in the 1960s?
a) McDonald's
b) Burger King
c) Wendy's
d) Arby's

Question 3: Which household appliance, introduced in the 1960s, made TV dinners even more convenient?
a) Microwave oven
b) Toaster oven
c) Electric range
d) Food processor

Question 4: What iconic fast-food item did McDonald's introduce in 1968?
a) Quarter Pounder
b) Big Mac
c) McNuggets
d) McFlurry

Question 5: What type of packaging innovation allowed TV dinners to be easily reheated and served?
a) Aluminum trays
b) Plastic wrap
c) Styrofoam trays
d) Wax paper

Question 6: Which fast-food mascot debuted in the 1960s as the face of McDonald's?
a) Ronald McDonald
b) The Hamburglar
c) Grimace
d) Mayor McCheese

Question 7: What drive-thru innovation, first introduced in the 1960s, streamlined fast-food service?
a) Two-way speaker systems
b) Digital menu boards
c) Curbside pickup
d) Order kiosks

Question 8: What frozen dessert became a fast-food staple in the 1960s?
a) Milkshake
b) Soft-serve ice cream
c) Sundae cups
d) Frozen yogurt

Answers: The correct answers are: 1. Swanson (b), 2. McDonald's (a), 3. Microwave oven (a), 4. Big Mac (b), 5. Aluminum trays (a), 6. Ronald McDonald (a), 7. Two-way speaker systems (a), 8. Soft-serve ice cream (b).

From Sputnik to Skylab: Early Space Missions That Made History

Question 1: What year did the Soviet Union launch Sputnik, the world's first artificial satellite?
a) 1955
b) 1957
c) 1959
d) 1961

Question 2: Which American astronaut became the first person to orbit Earth in 1962?
a) Alan Shepard
b) John Glenn
c) Neil Armstrong
d) Gus Grissom

Question 3: What was the name of NASA's program that aimed to land a man on the Moon?
a) Mercury
b) Gemini
c) Apollo
d) Voyager

Question 4: What spacecraft carried the first human to the Moon in 1969?
a) Apollo 10
b) Apollo 11
c) Apollo 12
d) Gemini 7

Question 5: Which space station, launched in 1973, was the first U.S. space station?
a) Skylab
b) Mir
c) ISS
d) Freedom

Question 6: Who was the first woman in space, flying aboard the Soviet spacecraft Vostok 6 in 1963?
a) Valentina Tereshkova
b) Sally Ride
c) Svetlana Savitskaya
d) Mae Jemison

Question 7: What major space event happened in 1971 with the Soviet spacecraft Salyut 1?
a) First space station
b) First reusable spacecraft
c) First spacewalk
d) First interstellar probe

Question 8: What program, launched in the 1970s, sent spacecraft beyond the solar system?
a) Voyager
b) Pioneer
c) Viking
d) Mariner

Answers: The correct answers are: 1. 1957 (b), 2. John Glenn (b), 3. Apollo (c), 4. Apollo 11 (b), 5. Skylab (a), 6. Valentina Tereshkova (a), 7. First space station (a), 8. Voyager (a).

Cinema in Technicolor: Blockbusters of the 1960s

Question 1: What 1965 musical, starring Julie Andrews, became a global sensation?
a) *Mary Poppins*
b) *The Sound of Music*
c) *My Fair Lady*
d) *West Side Story*

Question 2: Which 1963 historical epic featured Elizabeth Taylor in the title role?
a) *Ben-Hur*
b) *Cleopatra*
c) *Lawrence of Arabia*
d) *Spartacus*

Question 3: What 1969 Western, starring Paul Newman and Robert Redford, was a box office hit?
a) *True Grit*
b) *Butch Cassidy and the Sundance Kid*
c) *The Wild Bunch*
d) *The Magnificent Seven*

Question 4: Which 1968 science fiction film, directed by Stanley Kubrick, became a landmark in cinema?
a) *Planet of the Apes*
b) *2001: A Space Odyssey*
c) *Barbarella*
d) *Fahrenheit 451*

Question 5: What 1962 film starred Gregory Peck as Atticus Finch and earned three Academy Awards?
a) *To Kill a Mockingbird*
b) *Cape Fear*
c) *The Guns of Navarone*
d) *The Longest Day*

Question 6: Which 1961 musical won the Academy Award for Best Picture?
a) *The Sound of Music*
b) *West Side Story*
c) *Gypsy*
d) *Camelot*

Question 7: What 1966 Clint Eastwood film helped popularize the "spaghetti Western" genre?
a) *The Good, the Bad and the Ugly*
b) *A Fistful of Dollars*
c) *For a Few Dollars More*
d) *Hang 'Em High*

Question 8: What 1960 epic starring Kirk Douglas portrayed the story of a Roman slave revolt?
a) *Ben-Hur*
b) *Spartacus*
c) *The Fall of the Roman Empire*
d) *Julius Caesar*

Answers: The correct answers are: 1. *The Sound of Music* (b), 2. *Cleopatra* (b), 3. *Butch Cassidy and the Sundance Kid* (b), 4. *2001: A Space Odyssey* (b), 5. *To Kill a Mockingbird* (a), 6. *West Side Story* (b), 7. *The Good, the Bad and the Ugly* (a), 8. *Spartacus* (b).

Gag Me with a Spoon: Valley Girl Talk of the 1980s

Question 1: What 1980s slang phrase, popularized by Valley Girls, expressed extreme disbelief?
a) "No way!"
b) "As if!"
c) "Totally tubular!"
d) "Gag me with a spoon!"

Question 2: What term, often used to describe something excellent, was a staple of 1980s slang?
a) "Rad"
b) "Gnarly"
c) "Awesome"
d) All of the above

Question 3: What word, borrowed from surfer culture, described something very extreme or intense?
a) "Bodacious"
b) "Gnarly"
c) "Radical"
d) "Chill"

Question 4: What slang term referred to a good-looking guy in the 1980s?
a) "Hunk"
b) "Babe"
c) "Stud"
d) "Fox"

Question 5: What slang term was used to describe someone who dressed preppy or wealthy?
a) "Yuppie"
b) "Preppy"
c) "Richie"
d) "Trendy"

Question 6: Which Valley Girl slang term meant to calm down or relax?
a) "Take a chill pill"
b) "Cool it"
c) "Relax, man"
d) "Chill out"

Question 7: What phrase expressed agreement or enthusiasm, often sarcastically?
a) "Totally!"
b) "For sure!"
c) "You bet!"
d) "Duh!"

Question 8: Which slang term referred to a nerd or socially awkward person in the 1980s?
a) "Dork"
b) "Geek"
c) "Loser"
d) All of the above

Answers: The correct answers are: 1. "Gag me with a spoon!" (d), 2. All of the above (d), 3. "Gnarly" (b), 4. "Hunk" (a), 5. "Yuppie" (a), 6. "Take a chill pill" (a), 7. "Totally!" (a), 8. All of the above (d).

Tennis Titans: Grand Slam Champions of the Baby Boomer Era

Question 1: Which male tennis player won the first four Grand Slam tournaments in a single year in 1938?
a) Rod Laver
b) Don Budge
c) Bjorn Borg
d) Fred Perry

Question 2: What female tennis legend holds the record for the most Grand Slam singles titles?
a) Steffi Graf
b) Martina Navratilova
c) Margaret Court
d) Serena Williams

Question 3: Which 1970s player is known as the "King of Clay"?
a) Guillermo Vilas
b) Rafael Nadal
c) Bjorn Borg
d) Jimmy Connors

Question 4: What female player won the Golden Slam in 1988, capturing all four Grand Slam titles and an Olympic gold medal?
a) Chris Evert
b) Steffi Graf
c) Billie Jean King
d) Martina Hingis

Question 5: Which player, known for his fiery temperament, famously said, "You cannot be serious!"?
a) John McEnroe
b) Jimmy Connors
c) Boris Becker
d) Andre Agassi

Question 6: What was the name of the male player who won seven Wimbledon titles during the 1990s?
a) Pete Sampras
b) Andre Agassi
c) Boris Becker
d) Stefan Edberg

Question 7: Which female player defeated Bobby Riggs in the "Battle of the Sexes" in 1973?
a) Billie Jean King
b) Chris Evert
c) Margaret Court
d) Evonne Goolagong

Question 8: What legendary duo dominated doubles tennis in the 1970s?
a) Bob and Mike Bryan
b) John Newcombe and Tony Roche
c) Ilie Năstase and Ion Țiriac
d) Stan Smith and Bob Lutz

Answers: The correct answers are: 1. Don Budge (b), 2. Margaret Court (c), 3. Bjorn Borg (c), 4. Steffi Graf (b), 5. John McEnroe (a), 6. Pete Sampras (a), 7. Billie Jean King (a), 8. John Newcombe and Tony Roche (b).

Protests in the '80s and '90s: From Nuclear Disarmament to Globalization

Question 1: What movement, symbolized by a peace sign, protested nuclear weapons in the 1980s?
a) Greenpeace
b) Campaign for Nuclear Disarmament (CND)
c) Global Zero
d) International Peace Movement

Question 2: What protest, centered in Beijing's Tiananmen Square in 1989, sought political reform?
a) The Democracy Movement
b) The Cultural Revolution
c) The Student Movement
d) The Umbrella Movement

Question 3: Which 1990s protest focused on environmental protection, targeting logging in the Pacific Northwest?
a) Earth Day Movement
b) Save the Whales Campaign
c) The Timber Wars
d) The Rainforest Action Network

Question 4: What 1999 protest in Seattle targeted globalization and the World Trade Organization (WTO)?
a) Battle for Trade Justice
b) Anti-Globalization March
c) The Battle of Seattle
d) Free Trade Resistance

Question 5: What organization did Greenpeace activists protest by disrupting nuclear tests in the 1980s?
a) NATO
b) The French Government
c) The United Nations
d) The World Bank

Question 6: What was the central issue of the "Million Man March" held in Washington, D.C., in 1995?
a) Civil rights
b) Economic justice
c) Racial unity and empowerment
d) Voting rights

Question 7: Which iconic protest song became an anthem for anti-apartheid movements in the 1980s?
a) "We Shall Overcome"
b) "Sun City"
c) "Imagine"
d) "Blowin' in the Wind"

Question 8: What environmental protest led to the creation of Earth Day in 1970 and continued momentum into the 1980s?
a) The Clean Air Initiative
b) The Environmental Justice Movement
c) The Anti-Smoking Campaign
d) The Environmental Teach-In

Answers: The correct answers are: 1. Campaign for Nuclear Disarmament (CND) (b), 2. The Democracy Movement (a), 3. The Timber Wars (c), 4. The Battle of Seattle (c), 5. The French Government (b), 6. Racial unity and empowerment (c), 7. "Sun City" (b), 8. The Environmental Teach-In (d).

From Bush to Clinton: Shaping the 1990s Political Landscape

Question 1: Which U.S. president famously said, "Read my lips: no new taxes," during his 1988 campaign?
a) George H.W. Bush
b) Ronald Reagan
c) Bill Clinton
d) Al Gore

Question 2: What military operation in 1991 aimed to liberate Kuwait from Iraqi occupation?
a) Operation Desert Shield
b) Operation Desert Storm
c) Operation Enduring Freedom
d) Operation Freedom Strike

Question 3: Which 1993 agreement established a trade bloc between the U.S., Canada, and Mexico?
a) GATT
b) NAFTA
c) WTO
d) USMCA

Question 4: What 1994 initiative, led by Newt Gingrich, outlined Republican priorities for Congress?
a) The Contract with America
b) The Balanced Budget Act
c) The Conservative Agenda
d) The Grand Old Plan

Question 5: What domestic program did Bill Clinton emphasize during his presidency?
a) Welfare reform
b) The War on Drugs
c) The Great Society
d) The New Frontier

Question 6: What scandal involving Bill Clinton led to his impeachment in 1998?
a) Whitewater
b) Monica Lewinsky
c) Travelgate
d) Iran-Contra

Question 7: Which country did George H.W. Bush invade in 1989 to remove leader Manuel Noriega?
a) Nicaragua
b) El Salvador
c) Panama
d) Haiti

Question 8: What was the name of the 1992 independent candidate whose campaign impacted the Clinton-Bush election?
a) Ross Perot
b) Ralph Nader
c) Pat Buchanan
d) Bob Dole

Answers: The correct answers are: 1. George H.W. Bush (a), 2. Operation Desert Storm (b), 3. NAFTA (b), 4. The Contract with America (a), 5. Welfare reform (a), 6. Monica Lewinsky (b), 7. Panama (c), 8. Ross Perot (a).

Computing Power: From Room-Sized Machines to Personal Computers

Question 1: What was the name of the first general-purpose electronic computer, completed in 1945?
a) ENIAC
b) UNIVAC
c) IBM 701
d) Mark I

Question 2: Which company introduced the first commercially successful personal computer, the Apple II, in 1977?
a) Microsoft
b) IBM
c) Apple
d) Hewlett-Packard

Question 3: What graphical user interface (GUI) operating system did Microsoft launch in 1985?
a) Windows 1.0
b) DOS
c) Macintosh OS
d) Unix

Question 4: What 1990s technology became a global phenomenon for connecting computers via the internet?
a) World Wide Web
b) LAN
c) Bluetooth
d) VPN

Question 5: Which IBM computer, released in 1981, popularized the term "PC"?
a) IBM System/360
b) IBM 5150
c) IBM Model 1
d) IBM ThinkPad

Question 6: What breakthrough chip technology did Intel release in 1971, launching the microprocessor era?
a) Intel 4004
b) Intel 8086
c) Intel Pentium
d) Intel Core

Question 7: What 1960s computer programming language was one of the first widely used high-level languages?
a) COBOL
b) FORTRAN
c) BASIC
d) Pascal

Question 8: What online marketplace, founded in 1995, was among the first to capitalize on e-commerce?
a) Amazon
b) eBay
c) Craigslist
d) Yahoo! Auctions

Answers: The correct answers are: 1. ENIAC (a), 2. Apple (c), 3. Windows 1.0 (a), 4. World Wide Web (a), 5. IBM 5150 (b), 6. Intel 4004 (a), 7. COBOL (a), 8. eBay (b).

The Fall of the Wall: The End of the Cold War in the 1980s

Question 1: What year marked the fall of the Berlin Wall, symbolizing the end of the Cold War?
a) 1987
b) 1988
c) 1989
d) 1990

Question 2: Which Soviet leader's policies of Glasnost and Perestroika paved the way for the Cold War's conclusion?
a) Mikhail Gorbachev
b) Boris Yeltsin
c) Leonid Brezhnev
d) Vladimir Putin

Question 3: What U.S. president is famously associated with the phrase "Mr. Gorbachev, tear down this wall"?
a) Jimmy Carter
b) Ronald Reagan
c) George H.W. Bush
d) Bill Clinton

Question 4: What treaty, signed in 1987, significantly reduced intermediate-range nuclear weapons?
a) SALT I
b) INF Treaty
c) START Treaty
d) ABM Treaty

Question 5: What European nation was reunified shortly after the fall of the Berlin Wall?
a) Poland
b) Germany
c) Czechoslovakia
d) Hungary

Question 6: What symbolic action occurred on November 9, 1989, regarding the Berlin Wall?
a) Crowds began dismantling it
b) East Germany announced free elections
c) Soviet troops withdrew from Berlin
d) The wall was officially demolished

Question 7: Which East German city was most affected by the Berlin Wall?
a) Leipzig
b) Dresden
c) Berlin
d) Potsdam

Question 8: What Cold War military alliance dissolved in 1991, marking the end of Soviet influence in Eastern Europe?
a) NATO
b) Warsaw Pact
c) SEATO
d) The Axis Alliance

Answers: The correct answers are: 1. 1989 (c), 2. Mikhail Gorbachev (a), 3. Ronald Reagan (b), 4. INF Treaty (b), 5. Germany (b), 6. Crowds began dismantling it (a), 7. Berlin (c), 8. Warsaw Pact (b).

MTV Generation: The Birth of Music Television in the 1980s

Question 1: What year did MTV launch, revolutionizing music and pop culture?
a) 1979
b) 1980
c) 1981
d) 1982

Question 2: What was the first music video aired on MTV?
a) "Thriller" by Michael Jackson
b) "Video Killed the Radio Star" by The Buggles
c) "Like a Virgin" by Madonna
d) "Take On Me" by A-ha

Question 3: Which artist became an MTV icon with the music video for "Thriller"?
a) Prince
b) Michael Jackson
c) Madonna
d) David Bowie

Question 4: What MTV program, introduced in the late 1980s, showcased acoustic performances by top artists?
a) MTV Unplugged
b) MTV Live
c) Total Request Live
d) Rock the Night

Question 5: Which 1980s band is closely associated with the music video for "Hungry Like the Wolf"?
a) Duran Duran
b) The Police
c) Eurythmics
d) Wham!

Question 6: What award show, launched by MTV in 1984, celebrated achievements in music videos?
a) Billboard Music Awards
b) MTV Video Music Awards (VMAs)
c) Grammy Awards
d) People's Choice Awards

Question 7: Which artist's performance of "Like a Virgin" at the 1984 VMAs became legendary?
a) Whitney Houston
b) Cyndi Lauper
c) Madonna
d) Janet Jackson

Question 8: Which genre of music gained significant popularity through MTV during the 1980s?
a) Grunge
b) New Wave
c) Punk Rock
d) Hip-Hop

Answers: The correct answers are: 1. 1981 (c), 2. "Video Killed the Radio Star" by The Buggles (b), 3. Michael Jackson (b), 4. MTV Unplugged (a), 5. Duran Duran (a), 6. MTV Video Music Awards (VMAs) (b), 7. Madonna (c), 8. New Wave (b).

Road Trips and Route 66: Exploring America in the 1950s

Question 1: What nickname was given to Route 66 for its importance to travelers?
a) The Main Street of America
b) The Freedom Road
c) America's Trail
d) The Traveler's Highway

Question 2: What song, covered by Nat King Cole, made Route 66 famous?
a) "Highway to Heaven"
b) "Get Your Kicks on Route 66"
c) "Travelin' Blues"
d) "Road to Anywhere"

Question 3: What kind of roadside attraction was popular along Route 66 in the 1950s?
a) Diners and motels
b) Gas stations and billboards
c) Mini-golf courses
d) Giant sculptures

Question 4: What was a common family car for road trips during the 1950s?
a) Ford Thunderbird
b) Chevrolet Bel Air
c) Dodge Charger
d) Plymouth Barracuda

Question 5: What type of fast-food restaurant became popular stops on Route 66 in the 1950s?
a) Drive-ins
b) Dine-in cafes
c) Food trucks
d) Buffets

Question 6: Which state is NOT part of the Route 66 route?
a) Illinois
b) Arizona
c) Montana
d) Texas

Question 7: What government initiative in the 1950s began the decline of Route 66's importance?
a) The Interstate Highway System
b) The Federal Road Act
c) The Urban Freeway Plan
d) The Auto Infrastructure Act

Question 8: What nostalgic term refers to the 1950s culture of driving and exploring America?
a) Roadster Era
b) Car Culture
c) The Open Road Movement
d) Route Revival

Answers: The correct answers are: 1. The Main Street of America (a), 2. "Get Your Kicks on Route 66" (b), 3. Diners and motels (a), 4. Chevrolet Bel Air (b), 5. Drive-ins (a), 6. Montana (c), 7. The Interstate Highway System (a), 8. Car Culture (b).

Golfing Greats: Masters of the Green

Question 1: Who was the first golfer to win the Masters Tournament four times?
a) Jack Nicklaus
b) Arnold Palmer
c) Bobby Jones
d) Tiger Woods

Question 2: What golfer, known as "The Golden Bear," holds the record for the most major championship wins?
a) Sam Snead
b) Jack Nicklaus
c) Ben Hogan
d) Gary Player

Question 3: Which legendary golfer completed the Grand Slam in 1930?
a) Bobby Jones
b) Gene Sarazen
c) Walter Hagen
d) Harry Vardon

Question 4: What year did Tiger Woods win his first Masters Tournament, setting a record margin of victory?
a) 1995
b) 1997
c) 1999
d) 2001

Question 5: Who was the first non-American to win the Masters Tournament?
a) Gary Player
b) Seve Ballesteros
c) Greg Norman
d) Peter Thomson

Question 6: Which golfer was nicknamed "The King" and is credited with popularizing the sport in the 1950s and 1960s?
a) Arnold Palmer
b) Lee Trevino
c) Tom Watson
d) Billy Casper

Question 7: What iconic tournament, founded by Bobby Jones, is held annually at Augusta National Golf Club?
a) The PGA Championship
b) The Masters
c) The British Open
d) The Ryder Cup

Question 8: Who was the first African American to compete in the Masters Tournament?
a) Charlie Sifford
b) Lee Elder
c) Calvin Peete
d) Jim Thorpe

Answers: The correct answers are: 1. Arnold Palmer (b), 2. Jack Nicklaus (b), 3. Bobby Jones (a), 4. 1997 (b), 5. Gary Player (a), 6. Arnold Palmer (a), 7. The Masters (b), 8. Lee Elder (b).

Iconic Action Figures: From G.I. Joe to Barbie's Dream World

Question 1: What year was the G.I. Joe action figure first introduced?
a) 1959
b) 1964
c) 1971
d) 1980

Question 2: What company created the Barbie doll in 1959?
a) Mattel
b) Hasbro
c) Fisher-Price
d) Kenner

Question 3: What action figure, launched in the 1970s, featured the "Kung-Fu Grip"?
a) G.I. Joe
b) He-Man
c) Stretch Armstrong
d) Big Jim

Question 4: What 1980s toy line featured characters like Optimus Prime and Megatron?
a) Transformers
b) Thundercats
c) GoBots
d) Voltron

Question 5: What doll line, introduced in the 1980s, became famous for their unique adoption certificates?
a) My Little Pony
b) Care Bears
c) Cabbage Patch Kids
d) Strawberry Shortcake

Question 6: Which 1990s action figure line was inspired by a popular superhero team?
a) X-Men Figures
b) Power Rangers
c) Teenage Mutant Ninja Turtles
d) Justice League

Question 7: What toy, introduced in the 1970s, featured elastic limbs that could stretch several times their original length?
a) Gumby
b) Stretch Armstrong
c) Silly Putty
d) Bendy Bones

Question 8: What 1960s doll line introduced a dream house, cars, and a full wardrobe of stylish outfits?
a) Barbie
b) Tammy
c) Dawn Dolls
d) Miss Revlon

Answers: The correct answers are: 1. 1964 (b), 2. Mattel (a), 3. G.I. Joe (a), 4. Transformers (a), 5. Cabbage Patch Kids (c), 6. Power Rangers (b), 7. Stretch Armstrong (b), 8. Barbie (a).

Casual Fridays: The Rise of Comfortable Yet Stylish Clothing

Question 1: What 1980s trend introduced the idea of relaxed office attire on Fridays?
a) Business casual
b) Smart casual
c) Casual Fridays
d) Dress-down days

Question 2: Which clothing item, originally made for manual laborers, became a staple of casual wear?
a) Denim jeans
b) Overalls
c) Khakis
d) Turtlenecks

Question 3: What shoe brand became synonymous with casual comfort in the 1980s and 1990s?
a) Vans
b) Birkenstock
c) Converse
d) Skechers

Question 4: What fabric, introduced in the 20th century, became popular for casual and athletic wear?
a) Polyester
b) Cotton
c) Spandex
d) Wool

Question 5: What iconic polo shirt brand, featuring a crocodile logo, was a casual wear favorite?
a) Ralph Lauren
b) Lacoste
c) Tommy Hilfiger
d) Calvin Klein

Question 6: What was the name of the Japanese fashion brand that popularized casual basics in the 1990s?
a) Muji
b) Uniqlo
c) Gap
d) H&M

Question 7: What 1990s tech company famously adopted casual dress codes for its workplace culture?
a) Microsoft
b) Apple
c) Google
d) IBM

Question 8: Which accessory, popular in the 1980s, was a staple of laid-back, practical fashion?
a) Fanny packs
b) Scrunchies
c) Aviator sunglasses
d) Snapback hats

Answers: The correct answers are: 1. Casual Fridays (c), 2. Denim jeans (a), 3. Birkenstock (b), 4. Spandex (c), 5. Lacoste (b), 6. Uniqlo (b), 7. Google (c), 8. Fanny packs (a).

Scandals and Secrets: Watergate and Political Shocks of the 1970s

Question 1: What U.S. president resigned in 1974 due to the Watergate scandal?
a) Lyndon B. Johnson
b) Richard Nixon
c) Gerald Ford
d) Jimmy Carter

Question 2: What term was used for the secret group of operatives responsible for the Watergate break-in?
a) The Teflon Crew
b) The Plumbers
c) The Fixers
d) The Watergate Committee

Question 3: What major newspaper played a crucial role in uncovering the Watergate scandal?
a) The New York Times
b) The Washington Post
c) The Chicago Tribune
d) The Los Angeles Times

Question 4: What was the name of the secret informant who provided information about the Watergate scandal?
a) Deep Throat
b) Whisperer
c) Secret Source
d) The Mole

Question 5: What tapes revealed that Nixon had been involved in the Watergate cover-up?
a) The Pentagon Papers
b) Oval Office Tapes
c) Nixon Diaries
d) Presidential Phone Records

Question 6: Which vice president resigned in 1973 over unrelated corruption charges?
a) Spiro Agnew
b) Gerald Ford
c) Nelson Rockefeller
d) Henry Kissinger

Question 7: What congressional action began against Nixon before his resignation?
a) Censure
b) Impeachment proceedings
c) Recall election
d) Congressional inquiry

Question 8: Who became president immediately after Nixon resigned?
a) Jimmy Carter
b) Gerald Ford
c) Spiro Agnew
d) Ronald Reagan

Answers: The correct answers are: 1. Richard Nixon (b), 2. The Plumbers (b), 3. The Washington Post (b), 4. Deep Throat (a), 5. Oval Office Tapes (b), 6. Spiro Agnew (a), 7. Impeachment proceedings (b), 8. Gerald Ford (b).

International Flavors: When Tacos, Sushi, and Pizza Became Mainstream

Question 1: Which cuisine gained widespread popularity in the U.S. after World War II, starting with dishes like tempura and sushi?
a) Japanese
b) Chinese
c) Korean
d) Thai

Question 2: What Italian dish became a staple of American fast food in the 1950s and 1960s?
a) Pasta
b) Pizza
c) Risotto
d) Bruschetta

Question 3: What company helped popularize tacos and Mexican fast food in the U.S.?
a) Chipotle
b) Taco Bell
c) Del Taco
d) Qdoba

Question 4: What sushi roll, featuring avocado and imitation crab, became the gateway to sushi for many Americans?
a) California Roll
b) Dragon Roll
c) Philadelphia Roll
d) Rainbow Roll

Question 5: What Middle Eastern dish, made with chickpeas, became a popular vegetarian option in the 1970s?
a) Tatziki
b) Falafel
c) Tabouli
d) Baba Ghanoush

Question 6: Which global coffee brand, founded in the 1970s, popularized espresso-based drinks in the U.S.?
a) Starbucks
b) Dunkin' Donuts
c) Peet's Coffee
d) Costa Coffee

Question 7: What cooking style, originating in Korea, gained traction in the U.S. for its grilled meat dishes?
a) Bulgogi
b) Kimchi
c) Galbi
d) Korean BBQ

Question 8: What 1970s food trend involved raw fish marinated in citrus juice, introduced from Latin America?
a) Ceviche
b) Poke
c) Tartar
d) Carpaccio

Answers: The correct answers are: 1. Japanese (a), 2. Pizza (b), 3. Taco Bell (b), 4. California Roll (a), 5. Falafel (b), 6. Starbucks (a), 7. Korean BBQ (d), 8. Ceviche (a).

Beatniks and Beyond: The Countercultural Literature of the 1950s and 1960s

Question 1: Which author, a central figure of the Beat Generation, wrote *On the Road*?
a) Jack Kerouac
b) Allen Ginsberg
c) William S. Burroughs
d) Ken Kesey

Question 2: What poem by Allen Ginsberg became a manifesto for the Beat Generation?
a) *Howl*
b) *America*
c) *Sunflower Sutra*
d) *Kaddish*

Question 3: What William S. Burroughs novel, published in 1959, depicted the countercultural underworld?
a) *Naked Lunch*
b) *Junky*
c) *The Soft Machine*
d) *Queer*

Question 4: Which 1962 novel by Ken Kesey explored rebellion and conformity in a mental institution?
a) *One Flew Over the Cuckoo's Nest*
b) *Sometimes a Great Notion*
c) *The Electric Kool-Aid Acid Test*
d) *Of Mice and Men*

Question 5: What group of writers was known for its exploration of spirituality, drugs, and alternative lifestyles?
a) Beat Generation
b) Lost Generation
c) Romantic Poets
d) Modernists

Question 6: What term was coined to describe followers of the Beat Generation in the 1950s?
a) Hippies
b) Beatniks
c) Yippies
d) Bohemians

Question 7: What 1960s writer chronicled the countercultural movement in *The Electric Kool-Aid Acid Test*?
a) Tom Wolfe
b) Hunter S. Thompson
c) Timothy Leary
d) Jack Kerouac

Question 8: What bookstore in San Francisco became a hub for Beat writers and countercultural thinkers?
a) City Lights
b) Strand
c) Powell's
d) Shakespeare and Company

Answers: The correct answers are:
1. Jack Kerouac (a), 2. *Howl* (a), 3. *Naked Lunch* (a), 4. *One Flew Over the Cuckoo's Nest* (a), 5. Beat Generation (a), 6. Beatniks (b), 7. Tom Wolfe (a), 8. City Lights (a).

Environmental Awakening: The Birth of Earth Day and the Green Movement

Question 1: What year was the first Earth Day celebrated?
a) 1968
b) 1970
c) 1972
d) 1974

Question 2: Which U.S. senator is credited with founding Earth Day?
a) Gaylord Nelson
b) Edmund Muskie
c) Ralph Nader
d) Hubert Humphrey

Question 3: What major environmental book, published in 1962, is considered a catalyst for the Green Movement?
a) *Silent Spring*
b) *The Population Bomb*
c) *Our Plundered Planet*
d) *A Sand County Almanac*

Question 4: What agency was established in 1970 to enforce environmental laws in the U.S.?
a) The Environmental Protection Agency (EPA)
b) The National Parks Service
c) The Natural Resources Dept.
d) The Conservation Corps

Question 5: What oil spill, occurring off the coast of California in 1969, helped galvanize the environmental movement?
a) Santa Barbara Oil Spill
b) Exxon Valdez Spill
c) Deepwater Horizon Spill
d) Union Oil Spill

Question 6: What international agreement, signed in 1987, aimed to protect the ozone layer?
a) The Paris Agreement
b) The Montreal Protocol
c) The Kyoto Protocol
d) The Ozone Preservation Treaty

Question 7: What environmental organization, founded in 1971, became famous for its direct action campaigns?
a) Greenpeace
b) Sierra Club
c) Friends of the Earth
d) World Wildlife Fund

Question 8: What symbol, created in the 1970s, represents the concept of recycling?
a) The Green Triangle
b) The Mobius Loop
c) The Eco Wheel
d) The Conservation Circle

Answers: The correct answers are: 1. 1970 (b), 2. Gaylord Nelson (a), 3. *Silent Spring* (a), 4. The Environmental Protection Agency (EPA) (a), 5. Santa Barbara Oil Spill (a), 6. The Montreal Protocol (b), 7. Greenpeace (a), 8. The Mobius Loop (b).

TV's Early Days: Black-and-White Gems of the 1950s

Question 1: What 1950s sitcom followed the humorous life of Lucy Ricardo?
a) *The Dick Van Dyke Show*
b) *Leave It to Beaver*
c) *I Love Lucy*
d) *The Honeymooners*

Question 2: What long-running children's show featured a friendly cowboy named Buffalo Bob?
a) *Howdy Doody*
b) *The Lone Ranger*
c) *Captain Kangaroo*
d) *Romper Room*

Question 3: What anthology series, hosted by Rod Serling, debuted in 1959?
a) *Alfred Hitchcock Presents*
b) *The Twilight Zone*
c) *The Outer Limits*
d) *One Step Beyond*

Question 4: Which news program, hosted by Edward R. Murrow, was a pioneer in broadcast journalism?
a) *60 Minutes*
b) *See It Now*
c) *Dateline NBC*
d) *The Huntley–Brinkley Report*

Question 5: What show featured a mischievous young boy and his dog, Lassie?
a) *My Friend Flicka*
b) *Rin Tin Tin*
c) *Lassie*
d) *Flipper*

Question 6: What comedy-variety program, starring Jackie Gleason, popularized the catchphrase "And away we go!"?
a) *The Honeymooners*
b) *Your Show of Shows*
c) *The Jackie Gleason Show*
d) *Texaco Star Theater*

Question 7: What game show, hosted by Groucho Marx, included the famous phrase, "Say the secret word"?
a) *What's My Line?*
b) *You Bet Your Life*
c) *Truth or Consequences*
d) *The Price Is Right*

Question 8: What 1950s Western drama followed Marshal Matt Dillon in the town of Dodge City?
a) *Bonanza*
b) *Gunsmoke*
c) *The Rifleman*
d) *Rawhide*

Answers: The correct answers are: 1. *I Love Lucy* (c), 2. *Howdy Doody* (a), 3. *The Twilight Zone* (b), 4. *See It Now* (b), 5. *Lassie* (c), 6. *The Jackie Gleason Show* (c), 7. *You Bet Your Life* (b), 8. *Gunsmoke* (b).

Rom-Coms and Tearjerkers: Beloved Films of the 1990s

Question 1: Which 1990 romantic comedy starred Julia Roberts as a prostitute and Richard Gere as a businessman?
a) *Runaway Bride*
b) *Notting Hill*
c) *Pretty Woman*
d) *Sleepless in Seattle*

Question 2: What 1997 film about a doomed romance aboard a sinking ship became the highest-grossing film of the decade?
a) *Titanic*
b) *The Perfect Storm*
c) *A Night to Remember*
d) *Poseidon*

Question 3: Which 1994 rom-com featured Hugh Grant as a bumbling Englishman and Andie MacDowell as his love interest?
a) *Four Weddings and a Funeral*
b) *Love Actually*
c) *Notting Hill*
d) *Sliding Doors*

Question 4: In *The Notebook*-esque 1996 film *Jerry Maguire*, what line became an iconic expression of love?
a) "You complete me."
b) "You had me at hello."
c) "I'm just a girl, standing in front of a boy, asking him to love her."
d) "It's always been you."

Question 5: Which 1998 romantic drama starred Gwyneth Paltrow in a dual-timeline love story?
a) *Sliding Doors*
b) *Great Expectations*
c) *Shakespeare in Love*
d) *Emma*

Question 6: What 1995 movie, featuring Alicia Silverstone as a Beverly Hills teen, is loosely based on Jane Austen's *Emma*?
a) *Clueless*
b) *Mean Girls*
c) *Legally Blonde*
d) *She's All That*

Question 7: Which Tom Hanks and Meg Ryan film, released in 1998, revolved around a digital romance?
a) *Sleepless in Seattle*
b) *You've Got Mail*
c) *The Lake House*
d) *Message in a Bottle*

Question 8: What tearjerker about a relationship facing terminal illness starred Julia Roberts and Susan Sarandon in 1998?
a) *Beaches*
b) *Stepmom*
c) *Terms of Endearment*
d) *My Sister's Keeper*

Answers: The correct answers are: 1. *Pretty Woman* (c), 2. *Titanic* (a), 3. *Four Weddings and a Funeral* (a), 4. "You complete me." (a), 5. *Shakespeare in Love* (c), 6. *Clueless* (a), 7. *You've Got Mail* (b), 8. *Stepmom* (b).

Soda Wars: Coca-Cola vs. Pepsi Through the Decades

Question 1: What year did Coca-Cola introduce "New Coke," causing widespread backlash?
a) 1975
b) 1980
c) 1985
d) 1990

Question 2: What marketing campaign did Pepsi launch in the 1980s to target a younger demographic?
a) The Pepsi Generation
b) Pepsi Points
c) Pepsi Challenge
d) Pepsi Max

Question 3: Which soda company famously aired a commercial during the 1984 Olympics with the tagline, "The Choice of a New Generation"?
a) Coca-Cola
b) Pepsi
c) RC Cola
d) Dr Pepper

Question 4: What iconic Coca-Cola ad, featuring children singing, became a symbol of unity in the 1970s?
a) "It's the Real Thing"
b) "I'd Like to Buy the World a Coke"
c) "Open Happiness"
d) "Taste the Feeling"

Question 5: What brand introduced Crystal Pepsi, a clear version of its soda, in the 1990s?
a) Coca-Cola
b) Pepsi
c) 7UP
d) Sprite

Question 6: Which company released "Diet Coke," the first-ever sugar-free cola, in 1982?
a) Coca-Cola
b) Pepsi
c) RC Cola
d) Dr Pepper

Question 7: Which soda campaign invited consumers to collect Pepsi Points and win prizes?
a) Pepsi Challenge
b) Pepsi Stuff
c) Pepsi Max Rewards
d) The Pepsi Generation

Question 8: What seasonal Coca-Cola ad featured animated polar bears enjoying a Coke?
a) The Christmas Caravan
b) The Real Holiday
c) Arctic Adventure
d) The Polar Bear Campaign

Answers: The correct answers are: 1. 1985 (c), 2. Pepsi Challenge (c), 3. Pepsi (b), 4. "I'd Like to Buy the World a Coke" (b), 5. Pepsi (b), 6. Coca-Cola (a), 7. Pepsi Stuff (b), 8. The Polar Bear Campaign (d).

The Volkswagen Beetle: The People's Car Through the Decades

Question 1: What year did Volkswagen first begin producing the Beetle?
a) 1938
b) 1945
c) 1955
d) 1960

Question 2: What nickname is commonly used for the Volkswagen Beetle in Germany?
a) Käfer
b) Bug
c) Auto Klein
d) Volksauto

Question 3: Which decade saw the Volkswagen Beetle become a symbol of counterculture in the U.S.?
a) 1950s
b) 1960s
c) 1970s
d) 1980s

Question 4: What Disney movie series featured a sentient Volkswagen Beetle named Herbie?
a) *The Love Bug*
b) *Chitty Chitty Bang Bang*
c) *Car Talk*
d) *Lightning Bug*

Question 5: What key design feature made the Beetle stand out when it was introduced?
a) Rear-mounted engine
b) Four-wheel drive
c) Convertible roof
d) Electric motor

Question 6: In what year did Volkswagen end production of the original Beetle design?
a) 1995
b) 2003
c) 2005
d) 2010

Question 7: Which advertising campaign in the 1960s helped popularize the Beetle in America?
a) "Think Small"
b) "Drive Big"
c) "The People's Car"
d) "Go German"

Question 8: What modern version of the Beetle was introduced in the late 1990s?
a) New Beetle
b) Beetle Redux
c) Retro Bug
d) The People's Bug

Answers: The correct answers are: 1. 1938 (a), 2. Käfer (a), 3. 1960s (b), 4. *The Love Bug* (a), 5. Rear-mounted engine (a), 6. 2003 (b), 7. "Think Small" (a), 8. New Beetle (a).

The Energy Crisis: Oil, Inflation, and Global Economic Shifts

Question 1: What year did the first major oil crisis, caused by an OPEC embargo, occur?
a) 1967
b) 1973
c) 1979
d) 1982

Question 2: Which U.S. president implemented a nationwide speed limit of 55 mph to conserve fuel?
a) Richard Nixon
b) Gerald Ford
c) Jimmy Carter
d) Ronald Reagan

Question 3: What country was the primary target of the 1973 OPEC oil embargo?
a) United Kingdom
b) United States
c) Canada
d) Japan

Question 4: What term describes the combination of high inflation and stagnant economic growth that characterized the 1970s?
a) Hyperinflation
b) Stagflation
c) Recessionary pressure
d) Inflationary lag

Question 5: What year did the Three Mile Island nuclear accident occur, influencing energy policy?
a) 1975
b) 1977
c) 1979
d) 1981

Question 6: What alternative energy source gained attention during the 1970s energy crisis?
a) Solar power
b) Hydropower
c) Wind power
d) All of the above

Question 7: Which major Middle Eastern conflict contributed to the oil crisis in the late 1970s?
a) The Six-Day War
b) The Iran-Iraq War
c) The Yom Kippur War
d) The Gulf War

Question 8: What U.S. government agency, created in 1977, focuses on energy policy and development?
a) Department of Energy
b) Environmental Protection Agency
c) Federal Energy Commission
d) National Energy Council

Answers: The correct answers are: 1. 1973 (b), 2. Richard Nixon (a), 3. United States (b), 4. Stagflation (b), 5. 1979 (c), 6. All of the above (d), 7. The Iran-Iraq War (b), 8. Department of Energy (a).

The Junk Food Era: Chips, Candy, and Soda from the '80s and '90s

Question 1: What candy, introduced in the 1980s, featured a sour powder-filled lollipop?
a) Ring Pop
b) Warheads
c) Push Pop
d) Fun Dip

Question 2: What brand of potato chips launched the slogan "Betcha can't eat just one"?
a) Pringles
b) Lay's
c) Ruffles
d) Doritos

Question 3: What soft drink, introduced in 1985, was marketed as "the choice of a new generation"?
a) Pepsi
b) New Coke
c) Crystal Pepsi
d) Mountain Dew

Question 4: Which snack, introduced in the 1990s, was shaped like dinosaurs?
a) Bagel Bites
b) Dunkaroos
c) Teddy Grahams
d) Dino Nuggets

Question 5: What brand introduced "Lunchables" in the late 1980s as a pre-packaged meal option?
a) Kraft
b) Hormel
c) Tyson
d) Oscar Mayer

Question 6: Which candy, introduced in 1994, was known for its interactive "candy and toy" experience?
a) Kinder Surprise
b) Wonder Ball
c) Ring Pop
d) Push Pop

Question 7: What snack, introduced in 1964, became a childhood favorite with its cheese-flavored dust?
a) Cheetos
b) Cheese Balls
c) Cheez-Its
d) Goldfish Crackers

Question 8: What soda brand was introduced in the 1990s as a caffeine-free clear cola?
a) Sprite
b) Crystal Pepsi
c) 7UP Gold
d) Surge

Answers: The correct answers are: 1. Fun Dip (d), 2. Lay's (b), 3. Pepsi (a), 4. Dino Nuggets (d), 5. Oscar Mayer (d), 6. Kinder Surprise (a), 7. Cheetos (a), 8. Crystal Pepsi (b).

Make Love, Not War: The Hippie Movement and the Summer of Love

Question 1: What year is considered the Summer of Love, when hippie culture flourished in San Francisco?
a) 1965
b) 1967
c) 1969
d) 1971

Question 2: What neighborhood in San Francisco became the epicenter of the hippie movement?
a) Haight-Ashbury
b) Castro
c) Mission District
d) North Beach

Question 3: What iconic music festival, held in 1969, symbolized the countercultural movement?
a) Monterey Pop Festival
b) Woodstock
c) Isle of Wight Festival
d) Altamont Free Concert

Question 4: Which psychedelic rock band released the song "White Rabbit," a counterculture anthem?
a) Jefferson Airplane
b) The Grateful Dead
c) Cream
d) The Doors

Question 5: What drug, often associated with the hippie movement, was central to the counterculture experience?
a) Marijuana
b) LSD
c) Cocaine
d) Mescaline

Question 6: Who authored *The Electric Kool-Aid Acid Test*, a book chronicling the hippie counterculture?
a) Jack Kerouac
b) Ken Kesey
c) Tom Wolfe
d) Timothy Leary

Question 7: What phrase became synonymous with the hippie movement's emphasis on peace and love?
a) "Peace and harmony"
b) "Flower power"
c) "Love and unity"
d) "Good vibes"

Question 8: What symbol, popularized during the 1960s, became a universal representation of peace?
a) Yin-Yang
b) Peace Sign
c) Dove
d) Olive Branch

Answers: The correct answers are: 1. 1967 (b), 2. Haight-Ashbury (a), 3. Woodstock (b), 4. Jefferson Airplane (a), 5. LSD (b), 6. Tom Wolfe (c), 7. "Flower power" (b), 8. Peace Sign (b).

The Golden Age of Variety: Shows That Brought the Stars Home

Question 1: What popular variety show, hosted by Ed Sullivan, famously introduced The Beatles to American audiences in 1964?
a) *The Tonight Show*
b) *The Ed Sullivan Show*
c) *The Dean Martin Show*
d) *The Jack Benny Program*

Question 2: Which comedy duo starred in a variety show featuring musical performances and comedic skits from 1951 to 1957?
a) Abbott and Costello
b) Burns and Allen
c) Martin and Lewis
d) Laurel and Hardy

Question 3: What TV host became known as "Mr. Television" during the variety show's peak era?
a) Milton Berle
b) Sid Caesar
c) Johnny Carson
d) Bob Hope

Question 4: Which variety show featured puppet characters like Topo Gigio alongside live performances?
a) *The Texaco Star Theater*
b) *The Red Skelton Show*
c) *The Ed Sullivan Show*
d) *The Jackie Gleason Show*

Question 5: What long-running variety program, hosted by Carol Burnett, was known for its comedic sketches and parodies?
a) *Laugh-In*
b) *The Carol Burnett Show*
c) *The Smothers Brothers Comedy Hour*
d) *The Flip Wilson Show*

Question 6: Which 1950s variety program was known for introducing Elvis Presley to a nationwide audience?
a) *American Bandstand*
b) *The Milton Berle Show*
c) *The Ed Sullivan Show*
d) *The Steve Allen Show*

Question 7: What variety program featured musical acts and a trademark opening line, "Heeeeeere's Johnny!"?
a) *The Tonight Show*
b) *The Dean Martin Show*
c) *The Johnny Cash Show*
d) *The Bob Hope Show*

Question 8: Which Saturday evening variety show, hosted by Lawrence Welk, showcased dance, music, and a signature bubble machine?
a) *American Bandstand*
b) *The Lawrence Welk Show*
c) *Hullabaloo*
d) *The Arthur Murray Party*

Answers: The correct answers are: 1. *The Ed Sullivan Show* (b), 2. Burns and Allen (b), 3. Milton Berle (a), 4. *The Ed Sullivan Show* (c), 5. *The Carol Burnett Show* (b), 6. *The Milton Berle Show* (b), 7. *The Tonight Show* (a), 8. *The Lawrence Welk Show* (b).

Hollywood Gossip: Scandals and Behind-the-Scenes Drama

Question 1: Which Hollywood actress's mysterious 1981 drowning remains a widely discussed scandal?
a) Marilyn Monroe
b) Natalie Wood
c) Judy Garland
d) Grace Kelly

Question 2: What 1950s actor was killed in a car crash and became a symbol of Hollywood rebellion?
a) James Dean
b) Marlon Brando
c) Rock Hudson
d) Paul Newman

Question 3: Which 1960s film's production was plagued by on-set feuds between Elizabeth Taylor and Richard Burton?
a) *Cleopatra*
b) *Who's Afraid of Virginia Woolf?*
c) *Cat on a Hot Tin Roof*
d) *The Taming of the Shrew*

Question 4: What 1970s Hollywood director fled the U.S. after being convicted of a serious crime?
a) Roman Polanski
b) Francis Ford Coppola
c) Woody Allen
d) John Huston

Question 5: What iconic actress's death in 1962 sparked countless conspiracy theories?
a) Rita Hayworth
b) Marilyn Monroe
c) Audrey Hepburn
d) Vivien Leigh

Question 6: What major studio cover-up surrounded the career of Rock Hudson in the 1950s and 1960s?
a) Financial scandals
b) His sexuality
c) Ghostwritten scripts
d) Embezzlement allegations

Question 7: What Hollywood couple's messy divorce in 1960 became tabloid fodder for years?
a) Debbie Reynolds and Eddie Fisher
b) Elizabeth Taylor and Mike Todd
c) Joan Crawford and Alfred Steele
d) Frank Sinatra and Ava Gardner

Question 8: What 1990s actor caused chaos on the set of *Mission: Impossible 2* due to extreme demands?
a) Brad Pitt
b) Johnny Depp
c) Tom Cruise
d) Val Kilmer

Answers: The correct answers are: 1. Natalie Wood (b), 2. James Dean (a), 3. *Cleopatra* (a), 4. Roman Polanski (a), 5. Marilyn Monroe (b), 6. His sexuality (b), 7. Debbie Reynolds and Eddie Fisher (a), 8. Tom Cruise (c).

Super Bowl Commercials: Memorable Moments in Advertising

Question 1: What 1984 Apple commercial, directed by Ridley Scott, introduced the Macintosh computer?
a) "Think Different"
b) "1984"
c) "The Future Is Now"
d) "Revolutionary"

Question 2: Which iconic beverage brand featured a young boy offering a soda to a football player in the 1979 Super Bowl?
a) Coca-Cola
b) Pepsi
c) Dr Pepper
d) RC Cola

Question 3: What snack brand's Super Bowl commercial featured "The Cool Ranch Kid" in the 1990s?
a) Pringles
b) Lay's
c) Doritos
d) Fritos

Question 4: Which 2000 commercial, featuring a group of frogs, became synonymous with Budweiser?
a) "Wassup!"
b) "Frogs"
c) "Bud. Weis. Er."
d) "True"

Question 5: What candy brand's commercial famously showed a boy attempting to figure out how many licks it takes to reach the center of a Tootsie Pop?
a) Hershey's
b) Mars
c) Tootsie Roll Industries
d) Cadbury

Question 6: What car company's 2011 Super Bowl ad featured a young boy dressed as Darth Vader?
a) Ford
b) Chevrolet
c) Volkswagen
d) Toyota

Question 7: What brand's 1980 Super Bowl ad featured a "Mean Joe" Greene jersey exchange?
a) Coca-Cola
b) Pepsi
c) Dr Pepper
d) Gatorade

Question 8: Which tech company aired the first-ever Super Bowl commercial in 1980 featuring a young Bill Gates?
a) Microsoft
b) IBM
c) Xerox
d) Hewlett-Packard

Answers: The correct answers are: 1. "1984" (b), 2. Coca-Cola (a), 3. Doritos (c), 4. "Bud. Weis. Er." (c), 5. Tootsie Roll Industries (c), 6. Volkswagen (c), 7. Coca-Cola (a), 8. IBM (b).

Hollywood Headlines: Firsts in Film and Television

Question 1: What 1927 movie was the first feature-length "talkie"?
a) *The Jazz Singer*
b) *Steamboat Willie*
c) *Metropolis*
d) *The Gold Rush*

Question 2: What was the first animated feature film, released by Walt Disney in 1937?
a) *Fantasia*
b) *Snow White and the Seven Dwarfs*
c) *Pinocchio*
d) *Dumbo*

Question 3: What 1950s sitcom, starring Lucille Ball, was the first to be filmed before a live studio audience?
a) *I Love Lucy*
b) *The Honeymooners*
c) *Father Knows Best*
d) *Leave It to Beaver*

Question 4: What 1953 TV event was the first to be broadcast live coast-to-coast in the United States?
a) Dwight D. Eisenhower's inauguration
b) The Academy Awards
c) The World Series
d) Queen Elizabeth II's coronation

Question 5: What was the first color television program broadcast in the United States?
a) *The Ed Sullivan Show*
b) *Bonanza*
c) *The Tournament of Roses Parade*
d) *The Wonderful World of Disney*

Question 6: What film won the first Academy Award for Best Picture in 1929?
a) *Wings*
b) *The Broadway Melody*
c) *All Quiet on the Western Front*
d) *Cimarron*

Question 7: What was the first movie to gross $1 billion at the box office?
a) *Titanic*
b) *Jurassic Park*
c) *Star Wars: A New Hope*
d) *E.T. the Extra-Terrestrial*

Question 8: What was the first television network to broadcast 24 hours a day?
a) CBS
b) NBC
c) CNN
d) MTV

Answers: The correct answers are: 1. *The Jazz Singer* (a), 2. *Snow White and the Seven Dwarfs* (b), 3. *I Love Lucy* (a), 4. Dwight D. Eisenhower's inauguration (a), 5. *The Tournament of Roses Parade* (c), 6. *Wings* (a), 7. *Titanic* (a), 8. CNN (c).

The Great Train Robbery: A Daring Heist of the 1960s

Question 1: In what year did the Great Train Robbery take place in the United Kingdom?
a) 1960
b) 1963
c) 1966
d) 1969

Question 2: What was the name of the train targeted in the Great Train Robbery?
a) The Royal Mail Train
b) The Flying Scotsman
c) The Orient Express
d) The Midnight Express

Question 3: How much money was stolen in the Great Train Robbery (in 1960s currency)?
a) £2.6 million
b) £5 million
c) £10 million
d) £1 million

Question 4: Who was the leader of the gang responsible for the Great Train Robbery?
a) Bruce Reynolds
b) Ronnie Biggs
c) Charlie Wilson
d) Gordon Goody

Question 5: What was the name of the farmhouse where the gang hid after the robbery?
a) Leatherslade Farm
b) Greystone Farm
c) Green Gables
d) Whitehall Farm

Question 6: How many members of the gang were convicted for their involvement in the robbery?
a) 5
b) 10
c) 12
d) 15

Question 7: Which gang member famously escaped from prison and fled to Brazil?
a) Ronnie Biggs
b) Buster Edwards
c) Roy James
d) John Daly

Question 8: What film, based on the heist, was released in 1969 starring Sean Connery?
a) *The Great Train Robbery*
b) *The Anderson Tapes*
c) *Robbery*
d) *The League of Gentlemen*

Answers: The correct answers are: 1. 1963 (b), 2. The Royal Mail Train (a), 3. £2.6 million (a), 4. Bruce Reynolds (a), 5. Leatherslade Farm (a), 6. 12 (c), 7. Ronnie Biggs (a), 8. *Robbery* (c).

Don't Have a Cow: TV and Movie Quotes That Became Slang

Question 1: What animated TV character made the phrase "Don't have a cow!" popular?
a) Bart Simpson (*The Simpsons*)
b) Scooby-Doo (*Scooby-Doo, Where Are You!*)
c) Bugs Bunny (*Looney Tunes*)
d) Fred Flintstone (*The Flintstones*)

Question 2: What 1980s movie popularized the catchphrase "Wax on, wax off"?
a) *The Karate Kid*
b) *Ferris Bueller's Day Off*
c) *Back to the Future*
d) *E.T. the Extra-Terrestrial*

Question 3: Which 1990s TV sitcom popularized the sarcastic retort, "How you doin'?"?
a) *Seinfeld*
b) *Friends*
c) *Frasier*
d) *The Fresh Prince of Bel-Air*

Question 4: What 1980s teen movie introduced the phrase "Bueller? Bueller?"?
a) *Pretty in Pink*
b) *The Breakfast Club*
c) *Ferris Bueller's Day Off*
d) *Sixteen Candles*

Question 5: Which sci-fi film coined the term "I'll be back," said by Arnold Schwarzenegger?
a) *The Running Man*
b) *Total Recall*
c) *The Terminator*
d) *Predator*

Question 6: What 1980s action movie popularized the catchphrase "Yippee-ki-yay"?
a) *Rambo: First Blood*
b) *Lethal Weapon*
c) *Die Hard*
d) *Commando*

Question 7: What comedy show gave us the quote, "We are two wild and crazy guys!"?
a) *The Carol Burnett Show*
b) *Saturday Night Live*
c) *The Muppet Show*
d) *Laugh-In*

Question 8: What 1990s romantic comedy made the phrase "You complete me" a household term?
a) *Notting Hill*
b) *Jerry Maguire*
c) *My Best Friend's Wedding*
d) *10 Things I Hate About You*

Answers: The correct answers are: 1. Bart Simpson (*The Simpsons*) (a), 2. *The Karate Kid* (a), 3. *Friends* (b), 4. *Ferris Bueller's Day Off* (c), 5. *The Terminator* (c), 6. *Die Hard* (c), 7. *Saturday Night Live* (b), 8. *Jerry Maguire* (b).

The Challenger Disaster: A Nation in Mourning

Question 1: What year did the Space Shuttle *Challenger* disaster occur?
a) 1984
b) 1986
c) 1988
d) 1990

Question 2: How many crew members lost their lives in the *Challenger* disaster?
a) 5
b) 6
c) 7
d) 8

Question 3: What was the name of the teacher aboard the *Challenger*, who was part of NASA's Teacher in Space program?
a) Sally Ride
b) Christa McAuliffe
c) Judith Resnik
d) Kathryn Sullivan

Question 4: What caused the *Challenger* explosion shortly after liftoff?
a) A fuel tank rupture
b) An O-ring seal failure
c) A computer malfunction
d) A structural failure

Question 5: What state was home to the Kennedy Space Center, where the *Challenger* launched?
a) Texas
b) Florida
c) California
d) Alabama

Question 6: Who was the U.S. president at the time of the *Challenger* disaster, delivering a heartfelt address to the nation?
a) Jimmy Carter
b) Ronald Reagan
c) George H.W. Bush
d) Bill Clinton

Question 7: What investigation body was formed to determine the cause of the disaster?
a) NASA Advisory Council
b) The Rogers Commission
c) The Challenger Review Board
d) The Aerospace Safety Committee

Question 8: Which future NASA program prioritized safety improvements after the *Challenger* tragedy?
a) Space Shuttle Recovery Program
b) Columbia Accident Investigation
c) Shuttle Launch Safety Initiative
d) Return to Flight Program

Answers: The correct answers are: 1. 1986 (b), 2. 7 (c), 3. Christa McAuliffe (b), 4. An O-ring seal failure (b), 5. Florida (b), 6. Ronald Reagan (b), 7. The Rogers Commission (b), 8. Return to Flight Program (d).

Soda Fountains and Milkshakes: Sweet Treats of the Baby Boomer Era

Question 1: What classic milkshake flavor trio was famously known as "Neapolitan"?
a) Vanilla, Strawberry, and Banana
b) Chocolate, Vanilla, and Strawberry
c) Chocolate, Coffee, and Vanilla
d) Vanilla, Chocolate, and Mint

Question 2: Which soda fountain treat combines soda, ice cream, and syrup?
a) Ice Cream Float
b) Milkshake
c) Sundae
d) Egg Cream

Question 3: What was the name of the iconic Coca-Cola fountain drink mixed with cherry syrup?
a) Cherry Coke
b) Shirley Temple
c) Cherry Phosphate
d) Black Cow

Question 4: What dessert served at soda fountains was named after the day it was originally sold?
a) Milkshake
b) Banana Split
c) Sundae
d) Malt

Question 5: What piece of equipment, introduced in the 1930s, made milkshakes an American favorite?
a) Ice Cream Dispenser
b) Soda Jerk Machine
c) Electric Blender
d) Milkshake Frother

Question 6: What chain of restaurants popularized malted milkshakes in the 1940s and 1950s?
a) Howard Johnson's
b) Dairy Queen
c) A&W Root Beer
d) Baskin-Robbins

Question 7: What was a common term for soda fountain workers in the 1950s?
a) Soda Boys
b) Ice Cream Jockeys
c) Soda Jerks
d) Milkshake Makers

Question 8: What fruit-topped dessert, served in a tall glass, was a staple of soda fountains?
a) Parfait
b) Banana Split
c) Sundae
d) Ice Cream Float

Answers: The correct answers are: 1. Chocolate, Vanilla, and Strawberry (b), 2. Ice Cream Float (a), 3. Cherry Phosphate (c), 4. Sundae (c), 5. Electric Blender (c), 6. Dairy Queen (b), 7. Soda Jerks (c), 8. Parfait (a).

The Energy Frontier: Nuclear Power and the Quest for Sustainability

Question 1: What year did the world's first commercial nuclear power plant begin operating in Shippingport, Pennsylvania?
a) 1956
b) 1958
c) 1960
d) 1962

Question 2: What major nuclear disaster occurred in 1986 in the Soviet Union?
a) Chernobyl
b) Three Mile Island
c) Fukushima
d) Sellafield

Question 3: Which U.S. nuclear plant experienced a partial meltdown in 1979?
a) San Onofre
b) Diablo Canyon
c) Three Mile Island
d) Indian Point

Question 4: What country produces the highest percentage of its energy from nuclear power?
a) United States
b) France
c) Japan
d) Germany

Question 5: What is the term for using uranium as a fuel source in nuclear reactors?
a) Fission
b) Fusion
c) Enrichment
d) Moderation

Question 6: What alternative energy source has often been compared to nuclear power for its potential sustainability?
a) Wind
b) Solar
c) Geothermal
d) All of the above

Question 7: What international treaty aims to ensure that nuclear technology is used only for peaceful purposes?
a) The Nuclear Non-Proliferation Treaty
b) The Paris Climate Accord
c) The Global Energy Compact
d) The Atomic Energy Agreement

Question 8: What type of reactor, first developed in the 1950s, uses water to cool and moderate nuclear reactions?
a) Boiling Water Reactor (BWR)
b) Pressurized Water Reactor (PWR)
c) Fast Breeder Reactor
d) Heavy Water Reactor

Answers: The correct answers are: 1. 1958 (b), 2. Chernobyl (a), 3. Three Mile Island (c), 4. France (b), 5. Fission (a), 6. All of the above (d), 7. The Nuclear Non-Proliferation Treaty (a), 8. Pressurized Water Reactor (PWR) (b).

TV Families We Loved: From The Bradys to The Tanners

Question 1: Which TV family lived at 4222 Clinton Way in a blended household of six children?
a) The Bradys (*The Brady Bunch*)
b) The Cleavers (*Leave It to Beaver*)
c) The Partridges (*The Partridge Family*)
d) The Ricardos (*I Love Lucy*)

Question 2: What 1980s sitcom featured a widowed father raising three daughters in San Francisco?
a) *Diff'rent Strokes*
b) *Growing Pains*
c) *Family Ties*
d) *Full House*

Question 3: What animated TV family featured a dog named Astro and lived in the futuristic Orbit City?
a) The Flintstones
b) The Jetsons
c) The Simpsons
d) The Smiths

Question 4: What family sitcom, starring Carroll O'Connor, tackled social and political issues in the 1970s?
a) *Good Times*
b) *Maude*
c) *All in the Family*
d) *The Jeffersons*

Question 5: Which TV family included a dinosaur named Dino as their pet?
a) The Cleavers
b) The Flintstones
c) The Ricardos
d) The Addams Family

Question 6: What popular family sitcom of the 1980s starred Michael J. Fox as a conservative teen?
a) *Family Ties*
b) *Growing Pains*
c) *Silver Spoons*
d) *The Hogan Family*

Question 7: Which animated family, introduced in the late 1980s, lives in Springfield?
a) The Jetsons
b) The Flintstones
c) The Simpsons
d) The Griffins

Question 8: What sitcom featured a wealthy African American family living in Manhattan?
a) *The Cosby Show*
b) *The Jeffersons*
c) *Good Times*
d) *227*

Answers: The correct answers are: 1. The Bradys (a), 2. *Full House* (d), 3. The Jetsons (b), 4. *All in the Family* (c), 5. The Flintstones (b), 6. *Family Ties* (a), 7. The Simpsons (c), 8. *The Cosby Show* (a).

Cold War Conflicts: Spies, Space, and Standoffs

Question 1: What term describes the political and military tension between the U.S. and the Soviet Union after World War II?
a) Cold War
b) Iron Curtain
c) Red Scare
d) Proxy War

Question 2: What 1962 event brought the world to the brink of nuclear war?
a) Bay of Pigs Invasion
b) Cuban Missile Crisis
c) Berlin Airlift
d) Korean War

Question 3: What U.S. spy plane was shot down over the Soviet Union in 1960, escalating Cold War tensions?
a) SR-71 Blackbird
b) U-2
c) F-14 Tomcat
d) A-12 Oxcart

Question 4: What was the name of the wall built in 1961 to divide East and West Berlin?
a) The Iron Wall
b) The Berlin Wall
c) The Soviet Wall
d) The Checkpoint Charlie Barrier

Question 5: Which Soviet satellite became the first artificial object launched into orbit in 1957?
a) Sputnik 1
b) Vostok 1
c) Soyuz 1
d) Mir

Question 6: What Cold War espionage thriller by John le Carré featured the character George Smiley?
a) *The Spy Who Came in from the Cold*
b) *Tinker Tailor Soldier Spy*
c) *The Russia House*
d) *Our Man in Havana*

Question 7: Which treaty, signed in 1963, banned nuclear weapons tests in the atmosphere, outer space, and under water?
a) The Nuclear Test Ban Treaty
b) The SALT Agreement
c) The START Treaty
d) The INF Treaty

Question 8: What U.S. initiative, announced in 1983, was dubbed "Star Wars" and focused on missile defense?
a) Strategic Defense Initiative (SDI)
b) Patriot Missile Program
c) Anti-Ballistic Missile Treaty
d) NASA Space Shield Program

Answers: The correct answers are: 1. Cold War (a), 2. Cuban Missile Crisis (b), 3. U-2 (b), 4. The Berlin Wall (b), 5. Sputnik 1 (a), 6. *Tinker Tailor Soldier Spy* (b), 7. The Nuclear Test Ban Treaty (a), 8. Strategic Defense Initiative (SDI) (a).

Space Age Milestones: First Steps Beyond Earth

Question 1: What year did the Apollo 11 mission successfully land humans on the Moon?
a) 1967
b) 1968
c) 1969
d) 1970

Question 2: Who was the first human to travel into space in 1961?
a) Alan Shepard
b) Yuri Gagarin
c) John Glenn
d) Neil Armstrong

Question 3: What was the name of the first space station, launched by the Soviet Union in 1971?
a) Skylab
b) Mir
c) Salyut 1
d) ISS

Question 4: What U.S. spacecraft, launched in 1977, continues to send data from beyond our solar system?
a) Voyager 1
b) Pioneer 10
c) New Horizons
d) Galileo

Question 5: What was the first reusable spacecraft, launched by NASA in 1981?
a) Columbia
b) Challenger
c) Discovery
d) Atlantis

Question 6: Which astronaut was the first American to orbit the Earth in 1962?
a) Alan Shepard
b) Gus Grissom
c) John Glenn
d) Buzz Aldrin

Question 7: What rover, launched in 1997, was the first to successfully explore Mars?
a) Spirit
b) Opportunity
c) Pathfinder
d) Sojourner

Question 8: What treaty, signed in 1967, prohibited the militarization of outer space?
a) Outer Space Treaty
b) Moon Agreement
c) Space Non-Aggression Pact
d) Peace in Space Treaty

Answers: The correct answers are: 1. 1969 (c), 2. Yuri Gagarin (b), 3. Salyut 1 (c), 4. Voyager 1 (a), 5. Columbia (a), 6. John Glenn (c), 7. Sojourner (d), 8. Outer Space Treaty (a).

Enjoyed the Book? We'd Love Your Feedback!

If you had fun, we'd be so grateful if you could take a moment to leave a review on Amazon. Your feedback helps others discover the book and keeps us inspired to create more trivia challenges!